Say What You Mean and Get What You Want

Tricia Kreitman is the advice columnist for *Mizz* and *Chat* magazines. She has a degree in psychology and is a qualified psychosexual counsellor. Over the last few years she has worked closely with the Family Planning Association and the BMA, and is Vice-Chair to the board of Brook Advisory Centres for young people.

Tricia is married with two sons and has a continuing interest in sex and life skills education in schools. She regularly gives talks and conducts small group sessions in schools on a voluntary basis, and has used these as background research for her books.

She also has a passion for scuba diving, but isn't often able or allowed to indulge it.

SAY WHAT YOU MEAN AND GET WHAT YOU WANT

TRICIA KREITMAN

Illustrated by Jane Eccles

MACMILLAN

First published 1996 by Macmillan Children's Books
a division of Macmillan Publishers Limited
25 Eccleston Place, London SW1W 9NF
and Basingstoke

Associated companies throughout the world

ISBN 0 330 33396 8

Text copyright © Tricia Kreitman 1996
Illustrations copyright © Macmillan Children's Books 1996

The right of Tricia Kreitman to be identified as the
author of this work has been asserted by her in accordance
with the Copyright, Designs and Patents Act 1988.

3 5 7 9 8 6 4 2

A CIP catalogue record for this book is available from
the British Library.

Printed by Mackays of Chatham PLC, Kent

Contents

Introduction

This book is about real people with real problems. They've all got one thing in common: they're stuck in situations that don't feel right, comfortable or even safe – and they don't know how to get out of them.

To help me write this book, I asked the readers of *Mizz* and *Chat* magazines to tell me their stories. Most of the book is written from a woman's point of view. This isn't surprising considering that I am a woman, but it's also because girls and women seem to have particular problems in this area. I received hundreds and hundreds of letters about relationships, situations and habits that people had got into but now felt unhappy with.

Some of the things they told me were seriously scary, like the relationships that seemed to promise true love but turned into living nightmares. Other letters were about the kind of things that happen to us when we get confused between doing what we really want to do and doing what everyone else wants or expects from us. In those situations it's somehow always easier to go with the flow than to take control and change things. So you end up telling yourself that everything's all right really – shove your worries to the back of your mind and get on with it.

Thankfully things often turn out well. There's no point in being a pessimist for the sake of it. But the occasions I'm talking about are the ones when your worries turn out to be well-founded and you find yourself deep in a situation that gives you, and maybe others close to you, a load of grief.

This book isn't designed to put you off ever taking risks, nor is it a subversive attempt to turn you into a perfect, law-abiding citizen. What I do want is to help you grab some control in those awkward situations where keeping quiet means being unhappy, taken for granted, or abused.

Standing up for yourself, being assertive, and learning to say no are all vital skills for a happy and successful life. But they're not exactly something we're taught or even encouraged to develop as we grow up. Often adults don't like it when young people – particularly girls – say what they think and feel. Speaking out can get you accused of showing off or bossiness. But there's a difference between being bossy (or a bully) and asking firmly and clearly for what you want and what's right for you. It has a lot to do with other people's feelings, but most of all it involves respect for yourself.

As the agony aunt for *Mizz* and *Chat* I read something like 400 letters a week. That's over 200,000 letters in the last ten years. A few of them are wind-ups and some are hilariously funny, but the vast majority are from sad, worried and frightened people of both sexes. That's an awful lot of agony by anyone's standards.

People often ask me how I choose which letters to include in the agony columns. There's no easy answer to this, but I suppose two of the main deciding points are whether or not I can actually give some advice or information that would be helpful, and what I call the 'gut response' factor. Some letters have me jumping up and down in desperation. They're the letters from the people I want to grab by the throat and shout at. I'm not angry with them – but their situation drives me crazy. I want to yell, 'This can't go on!' or, 'Look what you're doing to yourself here.' That's how I felt when I read this letter:

Dear Tricia,
When I first met my boyfriend I'd never been out with anyone else (I still haven't) and was so very grateful

that a boy wanted to pay so much attention to me. All my friends thought he was great and he got on really well with my family, so I kept telling myself how lucky I was to have such a perfect relationship.

We are together nearly all the time and he's always saying how much he loves me. So what's wrong, you ask? Well, I feel stifled, and the longer it goes on the more scared I am that I'll never have any life of my own. He hates it when I go out with my friends and I can't even look at another bloke without him going on about how I fancy them. He keeps talking about getting married and spending our lives together and although my friends are all envious I just feel scared. I want to go away to college but he can't understand this and says I should just stay at home and go somewhere local.

Once or twice I've suggested cooling things off or having a trial separation but he's so upset I'm really scared he'll do something silly. I know I'm lucky and unappreciative but I feel so unhappy about it all. I do care for him and I don't want to hurt him, but I can't see any way out. Please help me.

Love, Jayne

Sometimes simply writing down the problem allows you to step outside of your situation and look at it objectively. I'm sure that most of the people who have their letters published on the problem page don't really need my answers – seeing what they've written down in black and white is often enough to make the solution to the problem obvious. I certainly hope that's what happened with Jayne. But we don't all have that opportunity, so many of us (yes, me included) still end up in situations that just don't feel right.

This book has really been written for people in those situations. There's no point in me going on for pages and pages telling you what you should and shouldn't do (even supposing I knew the answers), so I am going to let the letters I've received speak for themselves. I have provided some guidelines for getting yourself out of sticky situations and how to cope when things go wrong; there's a lot of information on your rights and resource addresses and telephone numbers at the back of the book. But most of all I want you to hear the voices of the people who write to me. Listen to what has happened to them and see what message it gives you about your own life.

To start off with, how do you feel about these situations?

I have one friend who always manages to make me do things I later regret. A few years ago she helped me through a bad patch and ever since then, whenever I'm with her I always end up spending more money than I intend to or doing things I don't really want to. She's much more extrovert than I am and much more popular. She's very irresponsible with money, constantly getting herself further into debt, buying things that she doesn't need and going out for meals etc. and blaming her problems on other people. She also has extremely high expectations of people and when I'm with her I always end up behaving like a real mug. She's good fun to be with and I don't want to lose her friendship, but I sometimes wonder if it's worth the hassle of maintaining it!

Sonia, aged 18

What would you do here? Do you think Sonia is right to complain about her friend? And, if so, is there anything she can do about it without ruining the relationship?

The first night I got off with Pete I didn't know much about him. He walked me home and came in and met my father. This made me feel important as no one had ever done that before. I saw him every day and within a fortnight I was smitten. Looking back on it now I'd say he made me feel pressurized to have sex with him, although at the time it seemed like it was all my fault. Even early on I started to find out a few facts about Pete that should have warned me off him. He was homeless, he dealt in soft drugs now and again, and also took them himself. He already had a kid to another girl and had just come out of another relationship with a girl who had had an abortion to him.

He had heaps of problems but I felt sorry for him. He managed to get himself temporary accommodation at a stop-over but was thrown out of there for drugs. I had a part-time job and gradually he started getting more and more of my money from me. I gave it willingly as he made me feel so sorry for him. My friends and family all told me he was bad news, but the more they said, the more I wanted to see him.

Rachel

Introduction

Have you ever ignored the advice of friends or family when they seemed to be criticizing someone you liked? If so, who do you think was right? Would you act differently the next time?

I used to have big arguments with my parents every day because they seemed to be against me all the time and I thought they were old-fashioned. One day after a row my dad was so furious that he shouted swear words at me and sent me to my room. I couldn't hold back my anger. I wanted to get my revenge on both of them and I was sitting at my desk where I'd been doing some project work when I saw this tube of glue. It was clearly marked 'Harmful if inhaled' but I didn't care. I knew it was wrong but I felt satisfaction at the thought that I was doing something to hurt my parents. I breathed it in. I felt guilty for a moment but I reassured myself by thinking that it wasn't my fault – they had 'made' me do it.
Nicole

Most people have done something silly at times to get back at someone else – but how do you think you would feel afterwards? Would you be more or less likely to do it again?

I went on holiday with my friend and one evening at the pub we met two older guys. After talking for a while we went back to their place and ended up playing strip poker and getting off with them. I wanted the bloke I was with to stop, so I asked him to and he did. Then he said we could go up to his room and talk, so his friend could stay with my friend. When we were there he started getting off with me again, but said he wouldn't go any further. I didn't like it and wanted him to stop again, but he just kept telling me not to worry. I was too scared to really do anything and I was worried without knowing why.

Becky

Becky seemed to like this boy – so do you think it really was unwise to go to his room? What would you have done? Would you have been prepared to leave on your own, without your friend?

I'm 15 and have been going out with my girlfriend for just over two years. She's the only girl I've ever been out with. I suppose I do love her, but lately things haven't been very good between us. Whenever we talk we end up fighting and it usually ends up my fault. I've suggested we break up for a while but she started crying and made me feel guilty for even suggesting such a thing. She's said she couldn't live without me, even though it would only be a trial separation.

Phil

Can you understand how Phil's girlfriend feels? What do you think Phil should do? Do you think they'll stay together?

When I first came to school my maths teacher seemed to be just a very friendly teacher. He started to rub my shoulders and back every time he saw me (like he did to every girl) and I didn't really care. But then it happened

constantly and he started rubbing my chest (but not anywhere private) so I began to feel uncomfortable. I told a couple of my friends and they watched out for me but it still got worse, to the extent that I was terrified to go to his classes and was having nightmares about him.
Kim, aged 12 – at boarding school

Do you think you have any right to complain about a teacher? If so, how would you do it?

Five years ago when I was 22, I was lucky enough to be in a very caring, loving relationship with John. He treated me well and respected me. We had fun together, never argued, but unfortunately I was foolish enough to throw it all away. I met Steve when I was on a night out with a girlfriend. I was instantly attracted to him, even though I'm usually a very faithful and trustworthy person when I'm in a relationship. I was soon to learn that it is a mistake to take lust as love. I knew I wanted him and I told John it was over. I lied, saying I wanted some time on my own and that I wasn't ready for a serious relationship, but I started going out with Steve straight away.

Only two dates later he proposed and for some reason I accepted. It was foolish because I knew it wasn't what I wanted. Even so I went ahead and at Christmas the engagement ring was on my finger. There was conflict between John and Steve when John discovered that I was getting engaged after only one week and having ended our relationship saying I wanted to be on my own. I felt really guilty and I'd never intended to hurt him, and I wanted to explain everything to him but I couldn't because I couldn't even explain it to myself. Instead when he confronted me I told him to get out of my life. I soon discovered that Steve didn't like any of my friends and I had to start making excuses not to see them. I realized I was being taken over.

Corinne

If you love someone, should you be prepared to give up everything for them? What would you do if your boyfriend/girlfriend tried to stop you seeing your friends?

The way out of some of these problems may look fairly obvious to you and to me, but nevertheless all of these writers are stuck. They are being pushed around by people and events. This book is designed to help them take control and get themselves unstuck or – even better – prevent them (and you) falling into similar situations in the first place.

Chapter One

But Everybody Does It
COPING WITH PEER PRESSURE

All your friends smoke, or drink, or lie to their parents about where they're going at night. You're not sure about this, but you know that if you don't join in you're going to be the odd one out. So what do you do?

Let's face it, saying YES is a lot easier than saying NO. If you weigh them up, on the YES side you want people to like you, you want to make people happy, and it's generally easier to go with the flow. On the NO side, things like being the odd one out, getting cold-shouldered by your friends or branded a coward or a grass all put you off saying no. It is not surprising that the finger of decision usually comes down heavily in favour of, 'Oh well, I might as well do it.'

It's a lot easier when you're a small child because if someone wants the red brick that you're playing with, you can just shout NO – and if that doesn't work, bang them on the head with it. But somehow, as you grow up, things get more complicated. Friends are pretty important – in fact they're vitally important, and we've all been guilty of judging the importance or the general niceness of a person by the amount of friends they have. So if you want people to think you're OK, you like to be seen with a gang of mates. And doing anything that might get you chucked out of that gang, or pushed towards the edges, feels decidedly uncomfortable.

But what happens when those friends start doing something that you don't like the feel of? How difficult is it to stand up and say NO and how easy is it to put off the decision for another day and just go along with it for a little bit longer?

Julie's Story

I had just turned 16 and never even kissed a boy, never mind anything else. (Everyone at school knew this because of a gabby ex-friend.) I was used to them calling me square. I was also very shy which didn't help. Anyway all my friends smoked and one morning I was really depressed so I asked one of my closest friends if she had any fags. After about three minutes of being in shock she said she had 20 that her mum had given her that morning. So at break I had a drag and I felt really good and clever, so I took a full one. At lunch I went and bought my own packet and a lighter.

A week later I had a serious asthma attack so I reduced the amount I was smoking from ten a day to three a day. It was difficult at first but I soon managed it. After a couple more weeks another friend came to me while I was shopping and asked me if I wanted to go to a party that night because her parents were going away for the weekend. I agreed because I didn't want to let my new reputation down.

When I got there a lot of people were already drunk so I started drinking and smoking. Two really gorgeous lads came up and offered me a couple of trips. Well I wasn't sure what they were so I took them and then bought some more. Within the next three hours I must have taken at least five and I didn't know what the hell I was doing. Some friends realized I couldn't go home like this, so they went across to the phone box and told my parents that I'd fallen asleep but I'd be back home by lunchtime tomorrow.

I didn't wake up next morning until 11.30 and I felt awful, so I had a fag and a drink and felt better. I caught a taxi home and went to bed. My parents kept insisting that I needed a doctor, but I told them it was just a migraine and after some persuading they believed me. The thing is I was badly scared and I knew I had to do something. Luckily I had just started taking drugs so it wasn't too hard to wean myself off them and the fags. Now I only smoke if someone gives me one. I still don't know whether it was pressure from my friends or school that made me start but I know that I've never been so frightened. Some friends who go to a different school had already warned me against smoking and drugs and now I wish I'd listened to them.

Julie felt like an outsider. Because a so-called friend had told everyone about her 'lack of experience' she felt that the rest of the group was laughing at her. She wanted to improve her image and make herself feel important so, by smoking and taking drugs, she was saying, 'Hey, look at me.' She was seeking attention.

WHY ARE GROUPS SO POWERFUL?

Whether you're dealing with a small group of friends or a whole crowd of people there are a few things that can be very useful to know.

1. Where a group exists, it's more comfortable being in it than out of it.

Julie was an outsider and she had to find a way to get into the group. Unfortunately she worried about (what she saw as) her lack of experience and tried to project a false image by being harder and tougher than she really was.

2. A group tends to pick on its weakest member.

Members of a group often pick on someone who seems a bit different. This might be started by one or two individuals who want to show off or gain power, or who perhaps feel insecure themselves. Other group members probably feel uncomfortable but still opt to join in the bullying (that's what it is), partly to enjoy the feelings of power and strength but also to avoid being victimized themselves. Suspicions that this behaviour is wrong or cruel are quickly suppressed because, after all, everyone else is doing it too. So it must be all right, mustn't it?

Julie felt that she was being victimized because people were calling her square and leaving her out of things. It's lonely outside the group and it's easy for fears to magnify. Her imagination was probably exaggerating the situation, but she thought everyone was talking about her. She felt she was being picked on, becoming a victim. Smoking and taking drugs gave her temporary self-confidence, but she could have escaped the role of victim in other ways. Taking up a sport or a hobby or developing a passionate interest in some topic that no one else knows much about can all make you feel more powerful. Groups, and particularly the bullies in groups, look for weakness and vulnerability in their victims and any show of strength you make, means you are less likely to be picked on.

3. Understanding what goes on in a group lessens its power.

Groups can exert strong forces and it's easy to get carried along with them. But if you can stand back and look at what is happening, it becomes simpler to make your own decisions. Julie got caught up with her hard drinking/smoking image, but, because of a couple of nasty incidents, realized that she was doing herself damage. She was fortunate enough to be able to understand what was happening and decide that her own health was more important than impressing her friends. Immediately the group lost its power. She became happier, with more self-confidence, and discovered that she didn't need an 'image' in order to be liked.

BEST FRIENDS

Sometimes a group only consists of two people. I've spoken to many young people who have gone to extraordinary lengths to keep their 'best' friend happy. Sonia was one of them.

Sonia's Story

I have one friend who always manages to make me do things I later regret. A few years ago she helped me through a bad patch and ever since then, whenever I'm with her I always end up spending more money than I intend to or doing things I don't really want to. She is much more extrovert than I am and much more popular.

She's very irresponsible with money, constantly getting herself further into debt, buying things she doesn't need and going out for meals, etc. and blaming her problems on other people. She also has extremely high expectations of people and when I'm with her I always end up behaving like a real mug. She's good fun to be with and I don't want to lose her friendship, but sometimes I wonder if it's worth the hassle of maintaining it!

I don't allow any of my other friends (most of whom she thinks are provincial nerds) to get away with treating me like this, but somehow she always manages to make me feel I'm in the wrong and she's right.

Recently we arranged to go on holiday together, but then I thought that I'd rather save the cash and put it towards moving out from home. I've never let her down before (although ever since I've known her she's been late to meet me, cancelled weekends at short notice, etc.), but when I told her this she said she was disgusted, hurt and angry with me, reminded me of what a struggle she'd had to get the cash together and told me there were lots of other people she could have gone on holiday with. And surprise, surprise, we're still going on holiday together, although her financial state is far more dodgy than mine.

We live in separate towns so tend only to see each other at weekends, usually when one of us stays over with the other. But we always seem to end up doing things to help her, like decorating to the early hours of the morning, or trekking from shop to shop to find the perfect shirt to go with her new jeans.

I know it's childish and ridiculous to compare other friends with this girl, but whenever I go to see any of my other friends who live away they always spoil me a bit, as I do them when they visit me. She always seems to treat me like 'one of the family', which is flattering in a way but makes me feel very used in others. I don't want her to have to pretend to me that she's feeling great when she isn't or anything ridiculous like that, but sometimes I feel it would be nice if she made a bit more effort.

Sonia, aged 18

Sonia started her story by saying that her friend had helped her through a bad patch so she felt she owed it to her to be especially nice and amenable. Yet she goes on to list all sorts of behaviour that would make most people feel pretty fed up.

So is it really all her friend's fault? Actually I can't help wondering how much Sonia is enjoying being a bit of a martyr. She certainly likes being able to complain about her friend, but I suspect that because her friend leans on her and has expectations of her, it also makes Sonia feel important and powerful. So, a lot of the time, she goes along with her friend's demands because it makes her feel good. Her subconscious is telling her she must be a good person if she puts up with these sorts of demands.

All good things come to an end and Sonia is now beginning to realize that the balance in this friendship is decidedly uneven. She enjoys giving, but not to the extent that her own life and needs are totally neglected. My prediction for Sonia and her friend is that there will be an almighty row. Maybe the friend will have a flash of knowledge and see what she's been doing over the last few years, but somehow I doubt it. The more likely result will be that Sonia simply stops seeing her. And both sides will be left feeling vaguely unhappy.

What else could she do? Well, any good friendship or relationship involves a bit of negotiation and compromise. It's important to listen to what the other person wants, but it's also pretty vital to put your own views. Keeping quiet, even for the sake of not upsetting the other person, only allows them to assume that you agree with everything they're saying. This quickly becomes a habit, so you can't really blame them if they stop asking for your opinion or forget to think about what you want. Some people can only negotiate by arguing, but rows are very stressful and energy-consuming, so developing a calmer method to get your own way – or at least achieve a compromise – is a valuable trick to learn.

Getting your own way

Suppose Sonia arrives at her friend's house on Saturday morning only to learn that the friend intends to spend the whole day searching for the perfect white shirt. To avoid argument Sonia goes along with it but inwardly fumes for the next 24 hours.

What she should have done was countered her friend's suggestion with one of her own, e.g. 'Actually, I was hoping we could go for a swim today', or, 'I'm feeling a bit tired and trekking round the shops doesn't really appeal, so how about curling up with a soppy old video?' This immediately opens the way for compromise. A morning's shopping might be followed by a swim or a good weepy video, with both parties feeling fairly satisfied. Alternatively, Sonia may end up giving in to her friend but with the understanding that next weekend it will be Sonia's turn to choose what they do.

If you find it hard to say what you want, it can help to write it down first. This helps you sort out your feelings and focus on what it is you want to change. The important thing to remember in negotiation is not to apologize for your own feelings. She's not saying sorry that she has to look for a shirt, and you don't need to apologize because you fancy a swim or a snooze in front of the telly. And it's also helpful, particularly among close friends, to allow each other the occasional power of veto – to let each other refuse to do a specific thing sometimes. So while you should always aim for compromise, if there's something that someone really can't stand doing, eating, watching, etc. then they should be able to say so.

WHEN NEGOTIATION ISN'T AN OPTION

Sasha was a fairly normal 15-year-old girl when a friend at school invited her to a special youth meeting at her church. Sasha was quite shy, a bit unsure of herself and didn't have all that many friends, so she jumped at the chance to do something different and meet some new people at the weekend. But she soon found she was becoming involved in a frightening and manipulative cult.

Sasha's Story

My friend belongs to a very special kind of church and she always seemed so happy about it that I was very pleased when she first invited me to join her there. Everyone welcomed me but they kept telling me things about how my family isn't really my family and that I should sacrifice my life to Jesus for the Church. I did make friends there but they kept telling me things that I believed were completely wrong, for example that all homosexual people are damned.

When I go to the meetings I often feel very scared and frightened and the kind of things they talk about give me nightmares afterwards. Yet I can't seem to stop going. I know my mum's very worried about me and says my friend is a bad influence, but I'm so very frightened that if I don't go to the meetings any more something terrible will happen to me and my family.

Sasha was lonely and vulnerable and therefore easy prey for this group. She was delighted to make new friends and find that her social life had taken a turn for the better. But she knew right from the start that some of the things she was hearing didn't square up with her own feelings. The group worked on her, making her feel wanted and needed, whilst telling her horror stories about what might happen to her and her family if they didn't accept the 'correct' beliefs. Sasha was becoming so scared that by the time she wrote to me she was almost thinking of running away or even attempting suicide in order to escape the pressures from both the church and her family.

I wrote back advising her to find another grown-up to talk to about this, preferably someone nearby who could be trusted and who could help her sort out her fears and worries. I also pointed out that although I wasn't any expert on religion I did feel that most faiths try to make you feel supported and secure and that any religion that tried to cut you off from your family and gobble you up, body and soul, should be viewed with suspicion.

Thankfully by the time she received my letter Sasha had already spoken to her aunt. She was so desperate she had to talk to someone and her aunt had listened at great length and then pointed out how this group of people were trying to take Sasha over. And how what had started out as being an exciting and enjoyable experience had now become overwhelmingly frightening. She told Sasha that she should stay away from them for a while and then see how she felt. Sure enough, after a few weeks, Sasha found the nightmares were getting less frequent and she was looking at things in a different light:

At first my friend kept ringing me up and asking why I wasn't going to meetings, and I was scared to answer the phone. My mum (who knew about it by then) told her off and said that I wasn't going anywhere with her. It was pretty scary and I felt pretty uncomfortable at school, but luckily it was soon the Easter holidays and things were easier. Then after a couple of weeks I realized that a lot of the things I'd been taking for granted about that group's beliefs didn't make any sense at all. I hadn't realized how much I'd been sucked in. But somehow when I was with them and they were all being so nice to me, everything they said seemed logical. I'm only glad that I managed to get out in time.

Sometimes your friendship or love for someone can lead you into very dangerous areas. Rachel met a boy who seemed different from any of her other friends and she found herself attracted by his air of danger. Her friends and family all knew he was going to cause trouble, but nobody realized how much.

Rachel's Story

The first night I got off with Pete I didn't know much about him. He walked me home and came in and met my father. This made me feel important as no one had ever done that before. I saw him every day and within a fortnight I was smitten. Looking back on it now I'd say he made me feel pressurized to have sex with him although at the time it seemed like it was all my fault. Even early on I started to find out a few facts about Pete that should have warned me about him. He was homeless, he dealt in soft drugs now and again, and also took them himself. He already had a kid to another girl and had just come out of another relationship with a girl who'd had an abortion to him.

He had heaps of problems but I felt sorry for him. He managed to get himself temporary accommodation at a stopover but was thrown out of there for drugs. I had a part-time job in a grocer's shop and gradually Pete started getting more and more of my money from me. I gave it willingly as he made me feel so sorry for him. My friends and family all told me he was bad news, but the more they said the more I wanted to see him. I felt important because he was 19 and I was only 16 and none of my friends were going out with someone this old.

One day he asked me for my mum's video card. He was going to go into the shop, get videos out and sell them for drugs. I was to report the card missing. I went home, told my mum I'd lost the card and she phoned the shop. Disaster struck. The lady in the shop recognized Pete from having seen him with me and I had to tell my mum how I'd given him the card. Mum phoned the police station, they picked him up and eventually the Drugs Squad came to our house and gave me my purse back, which I'd given Pete, and searched my room for drugs. They fired heaps of questions at me, although I knew nothing about the extent of his drug dealings at that time.

The next thing I knew, Pete was on the run from the police and I sneaked into town to meet him. My pal knew but said nothing. My mum thought I'd finished with him at this point. I gave Pete money when I saw him and started sending him money weekly. Eventually my pal got so upset that she phoned my mum and dad. I felt so guilty about what I was doing, but I couldn't stop seeing him.

Then Pete said that he had to get away, so I handed in my notice at my part-time job without telling my mum. We ran away but Pete immediately made it obvious that he didn't want me tagging along. I ended up on my aunt's doorstep asking her to take me in. Three days later I went home with no part-time job and having left school with no prospect of a full-time job either. The only reason I'd left school was because all Pete's pals were older than me, none of them were at school and I felt the odd one out.

Things settled down and I got a job. Then Pete

showed up in town and started getting more and more of my wages. All my pals were mad at me but I just felt Pete was my life. He had a way of getting to me. I put up with so much and put my family through hell, but he kept telling me that I would never meet anyone else and I believed him, so stuck with him. I didn't want to be lonely!

I soon found out that he was having an affair with another girl, but I stuck by him. Eventually he went on the run from the police again and phoned me up numerous times hassling me for money. I had had enough and I was suicidal. I phoned a youth counselling line and told them what had happened. They listened to me for what seemed like hours and arranged for me to see a counsellor regularly. Finally I found the strength to write Pete a letter finishing with him. He continued to hassle me but I kept slamming the phone down and didn't give him a chance to say anything. One day the calls stopped and I haven't heard from him for two years now.

I put my parents through a lot but I was naive and only 16. The experience made me grow up a lot quicker and now I've met someone who really cares for me. We're happy and plan to be married very soon.

Rachel recognized warning signs right from the beginning but she felt sorry for Pete. She probably felt she could help him and that all he needed was a little love and understanding. She was impressed by his age and air of experience, but his neediness also made her feel important.

All the time they were together, Rachel gave and Pete took. He paid no attention to her happiness and assumed it was his right to have her support him. Their relationship was totally out of balance. I doubt there was anything else she could have said or done to have made him treat her better. Luckily she managed to break away from him, but she will carry the mental scars for many years to come. Reading her story, it's easy to say she should have dumped him much earlier, but she didn't have the strength. She couldn't step to one side and see her situation through an outsider's eyes.

In this position, talking to a trusted friend or counsellor is invaluable. If Rachel had been able to tell someone what was going on, they could have explained to her how things seemed from the outside. She might not have listened but it would have given her an alternative view plus, more importantly, some much-needed support. For information about counsellors and counselling see the 'Resources' section.

WHEN SAYING NO ISN'T ENOUGH

Sometimes saying no, or not getting involved, still isn't the answer. If a group of friends or someone close to you is into some kind of behaviour which is so frightening or so potentially damaging that you can't cope with it on your own, what do you do? Telling or 'grassing' on them isn't going to make you popular. But is it a valid choice?

My best friend John has always been a bit of a loner and I know he finds it hard to cope in groups. I've got lots of mates but they're not so keen on John, though he and I are quite close. We tend to do things on our own at weekends and evenings, but at school he keeps himself to himself. I've tried including him in things but no one seems happy about it. Recently he's become very sad and he's started to say that he doesn't think it's worth living. I didn't take him seriously at first, but now I've discovered he's stealing sleeping pills from his mum and I'm really scared he's going to kill himself.
Richard, aged 16

I'm so worried about my boyfriend as he's really into drugs and raves. He's been raving for several years and he takes drugs almost every night. I'm so worried about

28

his health. It's getting in the way of our relationship and I just don't know what to do. I know his parents would go mad with him if they found out, but at least that might make him stop. Don't tell me to talk to him as he just says he'll give up when he's ready. But what happens in the meantime? I need to do something before it's too late and I would feel so guilty if anything happened to him.

Sammy

My best friend's on a perpetual diet. About six months ago her parents got really worried and took her to the doctor, who said that she was borderline anorexic. They kept checking what she was eating and she seemed to get a bit better. But I know that she's now getting much worse and she's lying to her parents. She doesn't eat any breakfast and she throws her packed lunch away and then tells her mum that she's had something to eat at my house on the way home. It's not as though she's happy either, as all she keeps on about is trying to lose weight. And she looks awful. I don't understand why her parents can't see what's going on. I don't want to tell on her but I'm really scared that she's going to get seriously ill if somebody doesn't do something soon.

Sandy

I have a friend who told me the reason why she was anorexic. I was pretty shocked and I didn't know whether it was true or not. It was something that had happened to her a long time ago. She asked me not to tell anyone and there's no way I would want to betray her, but it was something really bad and I kept telling her she should talk to someone else about it, but she never would. It was awful because I felt so uncomfortable; I really needed to tell someone and all the time her father was going on at her because she wasn't getting any better. He blamed her for the anorexia and accused her of trying to get back at her parents.

Ruth, aged 17

All these letters pose a dilemma. Should you take on the responsibility for someone else and inform on their bad habits or wrongdoings? Would you feel comfortable doing that? Telling an adult what's going on might help them get their act together and could even save their life, but it would risk ruining your friendship. And what would other people say if they knew that you had 'informed' on your best mate?

There's no easy answer to this, but I think you should be guided by your own level of anxiety. When you start worrying about someone so much that it interferes with your own life, then you need to find some way of resolving that anxiety. That could be by talking to the person (although often, as when Sammy asked her boyfriend about his drug-taking, that means they'll just say they'll stop when they're ready to) or it could meant taking things further and telling an adult.

It's often a good idea to talk this kind of thing through with your mum or dad. Sometimes they can help you see things in perspective and you might be reassured and see that whatever's causing the problem isn't as bad as you imagine. On the other hand they could second your thoughts and say yes, something needs to be done and hopefully they will help you do it.

If you don't feel you can approach your parents, you could try a teacher at school, or you could even talk to your friend's parents. Sandy's friend was known to have a problem with eating and yet her parents seemed to be ignoring the fact that she was getting worse and worse. Sometimes families cover up secrets or have other problems which prevent them facing up to reality. It needs an outsider to point to the problem and say, 'What's going on here?'

Ruth's friend was trying to hide some sort of dreadful secret, but all the time she was becoming more and more ill. It's pretty obvious from what Ruth said that while her friend carried this burden, she was unlikely to recover from her anorexia. Her father's attitude may have been part of it, but Ruth was placed in an intolerable situation where she felt she may have had the key to her friend's future health and happiness but she had been forbidden to use it. I would advise anyone in Ruth's position to talk the situation through with someone they can trust to keep things secret. Often this means that a teacher or even a parent isn't the obvious choice.

If you are thinking of confiding in a teacher or somebody else in a position of authority, it's worth asking them first whether they are prepared to offer you confidentiality. That way you'll know how you stand before you start telling them anything private.

If confidentiality is a problem there are other places where you can get help and advice, for example ChildLine or the Samaritans (see 'Resources'). You can also look in the phone book for local youth counselling centres, because even if you don't want to discuss the situation with them, your friend with the problem may be very grateful to have the information.

Chapter Two

But We Know Best
COPING WITH PARENTS

Do 'discussions' always turn into rows in your family? Do you find yourself having the same old argument over and over again? Do you feel your parents really understand how you feel? Do you understand how *they* feel?

I suppose coping with parents is the biggie. I mean, if you grow up being Mum's little treasure or Daddy's princess it's pretty hard to step outside that role and take on your parents on your own terms. Of course, some people never do and even though they may have super-powerful jobs and run homes and families, the minute they walk inside the parental home their shoulders droop and they turn into 'our little angel' again.

Some people manage to get through their teenage years without any major hassles, but a lot of the tension that does occur happens in the home. And once you've had a mega-row with your family it's pretty hard to find anywhere to hide. So learning how to handle your parents so that neither they nor you have to cope with the pain of a major falling-out must be a good idea, mustn't it?

What you have to remember is that parents are often living a nightmare life. They see the big wide world as a terrifying, shark-infested place that's out to get their little darling. So they end up insisting that you have to be in by 9 p.m. because if you don't, you might meet a man who'll persuade you to have a drink, spike it with vodka, offer you a dodgy pill or fag to dope you, have his wicked way with you (without a condom) and then take you for a ride on the back of his motorbike which, being stoned himself, he'll then crash, leaving you a paralysed, pregnant, drug-addicted, alcoholic, teenage mum-to-be. Sounds far-fetched? Well, perhaps you should ask your parents what some of their secret fears are.

Of course, there is a more laid-back approach. Some parents know how hard it is to be young. *Oh boy*, do they know – they probably tell you endlessly about their own seriously unriveting teenage years. They know you want to try everything and experience everything and they believe that by getting drunk a few times and discovering how seriously unpleasant it is to throw up for hours you'll decide that you're far happier sticking to Ribena. So you get involved in drugs a bit? Well, they can cope when the cops come round, and if there's trouble at school they'll be able to reassure your head teacher that you've really learned your lesson now. Honest. And if you get pregnant – well it's not the end of the world, you can always have an abortion. These are really, truly, open, liberal-minded, Guardian-reading mums and dads. And don't knock them because, just like the ones that want to lock you in at night by 9 p.m., they're only trying to do their best.

Jeanette's Story

I feel like I'm a prisoner in my own home. I'm 16 and I've just done my GCSEs, and you'd think that my parents would have let up a bit on me. But oh no. All they go on about is my future and how I've got to work and invest for that. They expect me to go to my room and work as soon as I get home, and if I say I haven't got any homework – for example after my exams were over – they don't believe me. I'm allowed to go out one night a week, usually on a Saturday, but I'm supposed to be in by nine, or 9.30 if it's something special.

This is obviously ludicrous because all my friends stay out much, much later than that. If I do go out they want to know where I'm going and who I'm going with. If they don't approve of a person they refuse to let me go. Often they phone up the places I'm supposed to be to check if I'm there. It makes me a laughing stock amongst my friends and of course I've found myself lying to them and getting people to cover up for me so that I can have more freedom.

They've always told me that I mustn't smoke and I mustn't drink and that I'll get into trouble if I do. They haven't said much about sex except to stay away from boys. Of course, I do smoke because all my friends do, but I make sure I suck lots of mints before I go home. And I drink but I'm quite careful not to go home drunk although once or twice it's happened. Luckily they haven't realized and I've just said I had a headache and gone to bed.

I've never had a boyfriend, though there is this boy I quite like and I think he likes me. The thing is I know he'll never ask me out because I have to be back at such crazy times. But if he did I think I'd do just about anything for him. I mean, they don't trust me, do they? So I might as well give them what they expect.

Jeanette, aged 16

As you can see, Jeanette's parents are very, very strict with her and lay down rules and regulations about how she must live her life. They do this because

they're scared of what might happen to her, and genuinely want the best for her in the future. In their terms they care for her and are being very good parents. But that isn't how Jeanette sees it. She feels they don't trust her and because of that she's more or less determined to do everything they've told her not to do.

In this situation you have parents and a teenager who are going along separate tracks, each thinking they're doing the best but both being totally unaware of how the other side feels. Sooner or later it will probably turn into all-out war and both Jeanette and her parents will suffer.

My parents always talk to me about everything. Maybe it was having older sisters but they knew what the reality of being a young girl was and when I had my first serious boyfriend they knew before I did that things were going to start turning sexual. I remember I was just 17 and my mum sat me down and said that she and my dad were a bit concerned and felt it was time I should go on the pill. I know I must have looked shocked, but she just went on about how my life was my own and I was free to make my own mistakes but they wanted to make sure I was safe.

I went with her the next day to the clinic and got the pill and of course, very quickly, I slept with my boyfriend. Looking back I feel a bit sad about it. Somehow it wasn't my decision to sleep with him, it was actually pushed on to me by my parents. Although it all ended quite happily I suppose I do resent it a bit.
Alice, aged 21

Alice's parents were far more liberal and it was great that they talked to her so much about all sorts of things. They were also sufficiently in touch with the reality of teenage life to recognize when her relationship was about to move towards sex. They were giving her the freedom to make her own mistakes while making sure she was safe. That's pretty impressive, yet still Alice was left feeling rather resentful as though something had been taken away from her.

WHO HAS THE POWER?

Many relationships revolve around power and control. The parent/teenager relationship is no different. Parents, because of their age and status in the family (and usually they've got what money there is) normally have the power. They expect to have the power and they also expect to be able to choose how to use it. But teenagers are young adults and they are looking to develop their own power and this causes conflict in the relationship. (More about this later.)

Looking at the examples above, Jeanette's parents have the power and expect to keep it. They want total control over their daughter. They're doing it for her own good, but they don't expect her to make any decisions. If you asked Alice's parents where they thought the control was, they'd probably say that they were giving it to Alice. They were handing over the responsibility, allowing her to make her own mistakes and live her life as she chose. But Alice doesn't experience it that way. Admittedly she's a lot happier than Jeanette, but when it gets to a vital point in her life, her parents step in and use their power to take control of the situation. She wasn't allowed to decide when she was going to have sex. She felt it was pushed upon her.

Another problem with the 'make your own mistakes' approach is that it can come over to the young person as a lack of caring.

My mum pretends I don't exist half the time. I say something to her but she just walks away into another room and talks to my younger sisters. If I ask her if she loves me she says, 'Well, what do you think?' I don't think she loves me at all. I really want her to notice me and give me some of the attention she gives my sisters. Also there are lots of things I'd like to ask her but I don't feel I can. I feel really lonely.
  Danielle, aged 14

It is possible that Danielle's mum really doesn't care about her and is genuinely failing in her role as a parent, but perhaps she's rather overawed by this young (and possibly moody) teenager her oldest child has become and is trying to give her space to sort things out in her own way. Again the mother may think she's doing her best but the daughter experiences it as lack of love.

THE COMPROMISE

I haven't got a daughter but I always wanted to make sure my son grew up understanding how things were from both sides. I also remembered how awful it could be being a teenager and was aware that there'd be a lot of pressure on him to join in with the things that I probably wouldn't approve of. Because he's quite strong-willed I suspected there'd be no point telling him not to do things, so I tried from quite an early age, well before he was a teenager, to talk to him about the kind of temptations he'd meet and what the inherent dangers might be. Sounds a bit like lecturing but whenever we watched TV together or a soap and something came up about under-age sex or drugs, etc. I'd try and talk to him about it.

Poor kid, I expect sometimes he thought I was crazy going on and on about all this stuff, but luckily he was always really chatty back to me and I think I've learned as much from his views as I hope he did from mine. As he got older he still talked to me, though not about things that were intensely personal to him, but he often asked me for advice about friends' problems. It was interesting that once or twice he made comments about things that I was sure harked back to what we'd said years back.

We still have rows – all families do – but I think (or hope) that we're close enough that he'd always come and ask me if there's a real problem. Or, if he didn't feel he could talk to me, he'd find someone else he could trust.

Dan's mum

40

My mother used to go on and on about smoking, drugs, sex and everything. It was pretty obvious what she didn't want me to do but I have to admit she never actually said 'Don't do' something. I used to think she went over the top but then when I was about 15 and some of my mates started having problems I realized that they weren't able to talk to anyone about it. Certainly their parents never said anything to them and a lot of them ended up in our kitchen talking to my mum.

No, I don't tell her everything about my private life and, to be fair, she tries not to ask too much. But I do know that if I was ever in big trouble I could go to her. She'd probably yell at me, but I'm pretty sure she'd help.

Dan, aged 16

This middle, compromise approach isn't easy. It's treading a narrow line between going overboard and neglect but sometimes it can work. It's certainly what I think parents ought to try working towards but, realistically, it isn't usually adults who want to make the changes. If your parents are giving you grief then it's likely that you're going to have to lead the way to a better relationship.

THE SHIFT OF POWER

A young child has very little power in the family. OK, they can cry, scream and have tantrums in Tesco, but in a healthy, functioning family the parent will still retain control. I say 'healthy, functioning family' because in some cases parents are so terrified by their children's tantrums that they do give in to them. This can be disastrous because a young child needs to know there are firm boundaries which he or she can push against. In their minds parents are supposed to be strong and invincible. How else are they going to protect the child from all the bogeymen out there? So if a small child finds his parents constantly giving in to him he's going to feel scared and insecure.

But when that child grows into a teenager he or she will start wanting to take more control. The teenage years are all about developing your own identity and breaking away from the family. In some families this is so easy and gradual that nobody really notices it. In others it's sheer hell for about five years. And some people don't make it until their 20s or 30s.

So it's natural for a teenager to start to pull away from the family and want to take on more decisions about their life. But this has implications for the rest of the family. For a start the acknowledgement that your child is turning into an adult means that parents may begin to think of themselves as old. This can be a cause for grieving. The mother may cry because she feels she's lost her little boy, but she's also mourning the loss of her own youth.

Even more dramatic, as children begin to leave home, the parents change from being parents back into a couple. In many families this is absolute dynamite because both mum and dad have to relearn their roles and find some way of being together

without the kids. It's not surprising that so many divorces happen during these years. While you are struggling to come to terms with adulthood, your parents are facing the anxiety of sorting out who they are and what they've got going for them.

COPING WITH OVER-PROTECTION

The natural urge of parents is to protect their children. Parents are very aware of dangers and they see each Nine O'Clock News horror story as something that could happen to their precious child.

Accepting that your parents genuinely do believe they have your best interests at heart will help but you may also need to develop a strategy to cope with their over-protection. Your parents are used to behaving as adults and regarding you as a child.

They're going to find it very hard to step outside that arrangement, so you have to make the running. In other words, if you want to be treated and negotiated with as an adult you have to show yourself to them in an adult way.

Take this problem, for example:

My parents are driving me insane because they are so over-protective. I'm 14 and they treat me like a 4-year-old because if I want to go out anywhere with my mates I always get twenty questions about where I'm going and I'm told to be in around half eight. I've got a younger brother and he's out later than me some nights. Please don't say they're worried and that they care about me. I know this but I think they're being a little too over-protective. It's really getting me depressed. Sometimes I even get called names for not going out and I'm beginning to think that life isn't worth living.

Bella

How could Bella go about getting her parents to ease off? Where is she going wrong at the moment?

Bella has a problem and starts off by stating it quite simply. But then she begins to verge into hysteria, implying that if her parents don't give her what she wants she might as well kill herself. I know she probably does feel like this when she's particularly down, but using this threatening kind of response gives out an image of immaturity. Instead of saying, 'This is a problem and I've got to find some way to

44

negotiate around it', she's more or less saying, 'If I can't have things my way, I'll kill myself.'

I suspect that when she tries to discuss this with her parents she gets very cross and makes all sorts of demands. They look at her and see an angry child. So they decide she must be kept under tight control. And the next time she wants something they're even more strict.

Bella has to break out of this cycle and that means talking to her parents as an adult. It may come as a shock to them, but it should do the trick.

STRATEGIES FOR NEGOTIATING WITH PARENTS

Step 1: Decide what you really want – and what you'd be prepared to accept.

Let's say the issue is about how late you can stay out. At the moment your parents insist you have to be in by ten. It's no good demanding that they stop setting a curfew time or just 'treat you like everyone else' without specifying what that means. Perhaps your real aim is to be allowed to stay out until midnight (or 1 a.m. if it's a special party), but what would you really settle for? Accepting 10.30 on one or two weeknights and 11.30 if it's a special occasion or a weekend would be a great improvement on what you already have. OK, it's not perfect but we're talking about compromise here.

Step 2: Research your subject.

I'm sure you know how the rows go in your house. You want to stay out late and they won't let you. You ask why they can't be like other parents and ease off a bit. And they point out that they aren't other parents and they don't intend to act like that. Situation stalemate. What you have to do is find out exactly what the rules and regulations are for your other friends – preferably friends whose parents your parents know. Don't just say, 'Oh well, they're all allowed to stay out as late as they like', because I'm sure it isn't as simple as that. Take a notepad and ask them one by one. Then write it down so you've got a list. You probably find that each family handles it slightly differently and while some are more relaxed than yours, some of your friends probably have other rules and regulations like being allowed out only on one night a week.

Step 3: Start the negotiation – avoid the time and place of your usual rows.

If normal family discussions about this take place in the kitchen and that's where you usually end up screaming at each other, then you've got to avoid the kitchen. If it's mealtimes (very common) and it usually ends with one of you storming off, that's what you have to avoid. A good tip is to say to your mum or dad, 'I'd like to sit down with you sometime and talk about your rules on staying out late. When would you be prepared to do this?'

Note that you're being polite but also firm. You're not making demands – you're asking them to set a time for something that will happen between two equals. Many parents may fall over in a dead faint, gobsmacked by this, especially if they're used to being on the receiving end of a screaming demand. They may say that now is a good time but if you know that the dinner's about to burn in the oven or your kid sister will arrive home from school any minute, then you'd be better to say that you think it will need at least half an hour and could you agree on some time in the next couple of days when you're less likely to be interrupted.

If you know that things always get very heated around this type of discussion then suggest you go out for a coffee and talk it over there. Offer to make it your treat and your mum will probably be so stunned she'll agree. Or ask her to come for a walk with you. The important thing is to move the location away from the usual trouble-spots.

Step 4: Put your case.

This is the tricky bit. It's vital that you keep your cool and you don't let the emotional temperature rise. Remember this is a meeting for negotiation, not to make demands. If you start off in the right way then your mum and/or dad are likely to follow. So take control and start by stating the situation, i.e. at the moment there are certain rules/constraints on how late you can stay out, but you are unhappy about them and as a result there tend to be lots of arguments. You are asking if they can work towards some sort of compromise with you so that the rows stop and everyone is happier. Hopefully they'll agree that is the current position and you can then go on.

Point out you know they have your best interests at heart and, if you can, say something about how good your relationship is in other ways (flattery never does any harm, particularly if it's true). Admit that you may have made demands in the past that they didn't feel were reasonable, but equally, you don't feel the current rules are acceptable. Then show them your research. Point out the arrangements your friends have. But BE TRUTHFUL. Don't bend the evidence to fit your case, because they may ring up and check.

Step 5: Offer something in return.

This is the 'give-to-get' principle. In other words you want something – and you are prepared to give way on something else in order to get it. So you make your first bid. You say how late you would really like to stay out, but suggest that it would only be on special occasions – or once a week – or that you would always ring up before you started home to save them worrying. Perhaps you'd promise to stick with particular friends or avoid a place your parents strongly disapprove of. The important thing is to offer something.

Step 6: Deal with arguments.

You may be lucky and they'll say yes straight away, but it's more likely that the response will be something like 'You're too young', or 'Not until after your exams' or even 'Don't be ridiculous.' Try to bear in mind that this is the parent inside them attempting to regain control. Acting like this tends to push you back into the child role where you end up making demands and being unreasonable. DON'T DO IT.

If they say you're too young then don't get cross, just say, 'Well, when will I be old enough?' If they say you're being ridiculous, keep calm and point out that you aren't being ridiculous, just trying to have a sensible discussion. If they simply refuse then accept it but say 'Right, what would you agree to?' Keep the negotiation open. That's the vital thing.

Step 7: Reach an agreement.

Hopefully if you follow these steps you will come to some kind of agreement. It may not be what you wanted but with luck it will be fairly close to what you were originally prepared to settle for. Once this agreement has been reached, say it back to your mum and/or dad simply and clearly so that you know they understand it and agree to it. That way there can be no confusion afterwards.

Finally, don't forget to thank them – and do pay for the coffee!

How to negotiate with parents

BE REALISTIC ABOUT HOW YOU MIGHT COMPROMISE. DON'T ASK FOR THE MOON!	**1.** Decide what you really want – and what you'd be prepared to accept.
CHECK OUT WHAT HAPPENS IN OTHER FAMILIES AND WRITE IT DOWN IN A LIST. BORING BUT VERY USEFUL!	**2.** Research your subject
MAKE AN 'APPOINTMENT' WITH YOUR PARENTS TO DISCUSS THE SITUATION. TRY TO MAKE IT SOMEWHERE QUIET YET PUBLIC WHERE YOU ARE LESS LIKELY TO ROW.	**3.** Start the negotiation – avoid the time and place of your usual rows.

POINT OUT YOU ARE TRYING TO AVOID FAMILY ARGUMENTS BY AGREEING ON MUTUALLY ACCEPTABLE RULES. SHOW THEM YOUR LIST. **KEEP CALM**	**4.** Put your case.
THE 'GIVE-TO-GET' PRINCIPLE. IT'S WORTH GIVING WAY ON SOME THINGS TO GET YOUR MAIN OBJECTIVE.	**5.** Offer something in return.
IF THEY SAY YOU'RE TOO YOUNG - ASK WHEN YOU WILL BE OLD ENOUGH. **KEEP CALM**	**6.** Deal with your arguments
REMEMBER TO SAY OUT LOUD WHAT YOU THINK YOU HAVE AGREED. THIS AVOIDS MISUNDERSTANDINGS.	**7.** Reach an agreement

WHERE NEGOTIATION FAILS

I can't emphasize too strongly how important the negotiation procedure is. It isn't easy but if you can get it right at this stage you'll find it works throughout your life; not just with parents, but with partners, bosses, friends – everyone. But some people can't manage it or simply don't know how to do it. And sometimes parents won't listen. They're not prepared to let their teenager step outside of the child role and take part of their adult portion of control. This can lead to severe frustration, and frustrated people can do some pretty desperate things.

Nicole's Story

I used to have big arguments with my parents every day because they seemed to be against me all the time and I thought they were old-fashioned. One day after a row my dad was so furious that he shouted swear words at me and sent me to my room. I couldn't hold back my anger. I wanted to get my revenge on both of them and I was sitting at my desk where I'd been doing some project work when I saw this tube of glue. It was clearly marked 'Harmful if inhaled' but I didn't care. I knew it was wrong but I felt satisfaction at the thought that I was doing something to hurt my parents. I breathed it in. I felt guilty for a moment but I reassured myself by thinking that it wasn't my fault, they had 'made' me do it.

From then on whenever I was exasperated, disappointed or sad I'd just come up to my room and comfort myself with glue. It didn't seem to be harmful at all.

One day I was so furious with my dad that even sniffing didn't help so I wrote down every swear word I could think of on a piece of paper. After all, why can't I swear if he does? I kept that piece of paper. Sometimes I would think, 'God, what the hell am I doing?', but I just kept on and on.

One day my mum found the sheet of paper with all the swear words on. She was bad-tempered for days and wouldn't speak to me. I felt sorry and eventually I apologized. Then she started crying and said, 'But why don't you realize? You think I'm nagging you all the time but I do it because I love you.' I started crying too and we talked to each other for a long, long time. She forgave me for everything and I know now how stupid

I was. I'd never do such a thing again. Things aren't always wonderful but I just find it much easier to talk to my mum now, so we tend to be able to deal with problems when they crop up.

Nicole, aged 13

Sandra's Story

At 17 I got into a relationship which my family were dead against. Gary was twelve years older and not long out of prison. My family tried to split us up but I rebelled and went to live with him. My mum didn't speak to me for nearly eighteen months and it was me who made the first move and even then we only saw one another once a month. But my life was never as nice as I made out to her.

I soon saw the real Gary; violent, drunk and always in the police station. I was always very scared as I knew when he came home there'd be trouble and he'd hit me or worse. Yet I couldn't go home to Mum and admit I'd made the worst mistake in my life. She always said he was wrong for me and that I'd end up going back home, so there wasn't a chance that I would give in to it. I insisted on trying to prove her wrong even though I was scared.

In the end I took an overdose but I was found and taken to our local accident unit. Even after I was pumped out I was warned that I might not survive, but I did. Finally I was able to tell the doctor what had happened and people came to talk to me in the hospital, and arrangements were made to keep him away from me. It wasn't easy and I often had to call the police in, but I did manage to get away. About twelve months later Gary married a 16-year-old girl who I believe is having the same problems as I did.

As for me, I've got a new flat with a wonderful boyfriend and a beautiful baby daughter. My mum still doesn't know about the overdose or the reality of my life with Gary. But I feel that if she hadn't pushed me I would never have got into the mess I did. And now I'm learning through my own pain and I swear that as my daughter and other children grow up I won't interfere as my mum did. If anyone else feels as I did I would advise them to talk about it and not consider trying to kill themselves. I had a second chance, but not everyone is so lucky.

Sandra, aged 23

Julie's Story

My father is a minister at the local church and my mother helps with Sunday School, so when I stopped going to church they were devastated. They gave me a month as they thought it was a phase, but I soon realized that church wasn't for me and I'd only been going to please them. Well, my dad started saying that I couldn't go out until I started going back to church, so I left home for a couple of nights. When I went back they were much nicer to me – until Sunday came round again. Then it was back to normal and they started keeping me in my own room, so again I left home, but this time for a week.

It wasn't too bad for the first few nights as I slept at different friends' houses and then in the local bus station where it was cold but dry. When I went back home they were great, but that lasted only until the next Sunday, so I left yet again. One of the men at work told me to go back home and reason with them. Deep down I knew he was right, but I told him to mind his own business. I was back on the streets. I'd made a few friends but I was finding it really difficult to manage on the Youth Training wage.

One night at about midnight I was just settling down in the bus station when a boy came along. He looked about 20 and he asked me why I was sleeping there, so I told him everything. He said I was lucky to be able to go home as he couldn't since his mother was dead and his father hit him and abused him. When I asked him how old he was he said 17. I realized how lucky I am and caught a taxi home immediately. I reasoned with my parents and came to an agreement that I didn't have to go to any services, just help with Sunday School every so often. I owe a lot to that boy and really wish I could help him.

Julie, aged 17

Nicole sniffed glue to get back at her parents, Sandra put up with a violent relationship rather than risk her mum saying 'I told you so', and Julie ran away to escape her strict parents.

All three of these girls were desperate and they made decisions and took actions they later regretted. They came to terms with it in different ways. It's interesting that Julie finally managed to go back and negotiate with her parents. If she'd been able to do that at the beginning she'd have saved herself, and them, a lot of pain. Like Nicole, the other two were doing things to spite their parents. They didn't care if it was hurting themselves so long as it was plain revenge on their mums and dads. This is a natural human emotion but it's also a very childish urge. Remember what I was saying earlier about stepping out of the child role and taking some of the adult portion of control? Well, these three weren't doing that. Their behaviour wasn't driven by sensible planning or negotiation but simply by the urge to spite someone else.

Luckily, they all survived and Nicole and Julie developed better, if not perfect, relationships with their parents. Sandra is happy but I guess she still has a very distant relationship with her mum and misses her a lot deep down. After all, if you didn't want your mum to be nice to you, you wouldn't be so upset when she wasn't, would you? I hope Sandra can make better peace with her mum one day and maybe admit some of her own mistakes. It would clear the air and allow them to develop a more grown-up and equal relationship.

One thing all of them could have done when the problems first started was to get some advice from someone outside the family. If they didn't feel comfortable talking to their parents then they should have found another adult to confide in. This may seem impossible, particularly if you're convinced that the whole world is against you, but whether you talk to a teacher or a friend's mum or a relation, or even your mum's best friend, you can nearly always get some help. If you're scared that they are going to 'tell on you', then test the water first by asking if you can talk to them in private about something.

You can also phone one of the young people's helplines, e.g. ChildLine or the NSPCC, or contact a youth counsellor at your nearest youth advisory centre. Your library often has details of these and you can find more information in the phone book. See the 'Resources' section too.

COPING WITH PARENTS' PROBLEMS

Sometimes it isn't just a case of parents giving you grief, but of them suffering grief themselves. A typical case is where their relationship is starting to go wrong, or they've already broken up. Both parents can be consumed with anger and self-pity and may lay a heavy burden on their teenage kids. Helping them at home, particularly with younger brothers and sisters, is physically exhausting, but if they start telling you all their problems and expect you to support them through each major trauma you can also be emotionally drained.

I'm 13 and my parents have just got divorced. I'm living with my mum and her boyfriend. He's the problem as he seems to think he can rule my life. He's also taken over my mum so that she seems to think I'm nobody and isn't paying any attention to me. If he's nasty to me then I stick up for myself, but she backs him up and tells me to get lost.
      Lorna

My problem is my dad. He's always been moody but now he hasn't spoken to any of us for about six months. My mum tries to talk to him but he either doesn't answer or starts an argument with her. She hates him and tells me that if there was somewhere for her to go she would. It's only because of us that she doesn't walk out. Sometimes I wish she would walk out instead of dumping all her problems onto me while I'm meant to be working for my exams.

My dad can't bear to be in the same room as us. He buys his own food and puts his name on it and argues that my mum doesn't feed him. He calls me and her names, and I can't have friends round because he insults them. I've tried phoning ChildLine but I'm scared they'll trace the call and it won't be confidential. I don't even suppose they'll believe me.

Leigh, aged 16

I feel like killing myself or running away from home, but I haven't got the guts. The problem is my father. He's an alcoholic and has been for as long as I an remember. I can remember being 3 or 4, sitting on the sofa crying while my parents argued or fought. Now when he comes home drunk I can't cry in front of him or my mum, but I have to cry secretly in my room. He always upsets me whether he's drunk or not. I feel that he hates me. My mum does everything she can for me and my brother, but I'm always so scared of what he's going to do next and it worries me if she's in the house alone with him. I really want to

BOOKS
NEED
RETURNING
ON

12th

Dec

2016.

leave but I'm scared of what might happen if I'm not there.
Helen, aged 16

I think my family is going crazy. My mum and dad haven't got on for years and, a while ago, Dad was made redundant. He started going down the pub and drinking heavily. My mum had a part-time job and soon she was out of the house all the time. Then it became obvious she was having an affair with someone. My dad found out and almost killed her. The police came but nothing happened. It's just so sad when I see them and I've tried talking to my dad and asking what the hell he's doing to himself because I'm sure if he could only pull himself together things would get better. But he doesn't want to know. He says I'm being nosy and tells me to get out of his life. I wish I could just walk away from the lot of them.
Jonathan, aged 17

These people are caught up in their parents' mess. They love them and they hate seeing them with problems, so they try to take some of the burden and save them. Lorna is probably the most honest because she says that she misses the attention her mum used to pay her. She feels neglected and, in fact, she probably is a bit neglected. Her mum is certainly caught up in her new love affair, which must be a welcome relief after the trauma of her divorce, but somewhere along the line poor little Lorna gets missed out.

Leigh knows that her father's behaviour isn't normal. And she also realizes that her mum is adding to it by dumping the problems on her. She desperately wants somebody to take some of the pain away and I only wish she could find the courage to ring ChildLine. By the way Leigh, if you're reading this, ChildLine won't try to trace you and nothing appears on your phone bill to say that you've called them. See 'Resources' for more information.

Helen and Jonathan are both facing up to the fact that their dads are alcoholics and, while they want to get out, they're scared of what will happen if they're not there keeping the peace. It's an impossible situation because they're sucked in to this gigantic mess. If they break away they'll feel guilty and if they hang on in there, their lives could be ruined.

These are all situations where it is vital to get help. The bottom line is that the children of a family shouldn't and can't be expected to cope with their parents' problems. Of course the fact is that many of them do – and cope very well, but it's at tremendous cost to them themselves. Parents don't realize the burden they're putting on their kids so if you feel you're in this kind of situation then find someone to talk to. ChildLine and the NSPCC Helpline can help. Jonathan and Helen would also get very sensible support and advice from the Al Anon Family Association (see 'Resources').

By asking for help you are again taking some of the control. You're stopping being a victim, and reaching out and saying you need someone to give you a hand here. Often it's the teenager in the family who sees the truth of the situation and goes to get help, leading the way for the others.

For example, if Leigh told her mum that she couldn't stick things and she was talking to a counsellor then her mum might face up to the fact that it was time something needed to be done. Leigh's counsellor could find her mum someone to talk to and eventually her dad's serious mental problem might be acknowledged. Of course nobody can force him to have treatment himself, but the rest of the family could get together to make their own lives without him.

Some people take a great pride in trying to manage on their own. But asking for help isn't a sign of weakness. Sometimes it's the hardest thing to do. It takes courage and strength and is the first step on the road out of wherever it is you are stuck.

Chapter Three

Love, Lust and Loneliness
DIFFERENCES AND DIFFICULTIES

What is love and what is lust? Can you tell the difference? Often I get very confused and, judging from the letters I receive, I'm not the only one. All the same, I sometimes think it would be useful if we could label feelings one way or the other so that we knew what we were dealing with.

According to my dictionary, *love* means, 'Warm affection, liking and sexual affection or desire.' Sounds a bit airy-fairy to me. With *lust* at least the dictionary is aware of gutsier emotions: 'Animal desire for sex.'

So maybe in basic terms lust is fancying the pants off someone and love is the finer side of those emotions. I suspect they overlap a fair amount – and where you get both it's downright mind-blowing.

LOVE **WOW!** LUST

CONFUSING LUST AND LOVE

When I get letters from girls saying they're desperately in love with a boy who doesn't even know they exist, is it really love or is it lust? And can you love someone that you don't actually fancy?

Maybe all that seems a bit theoretical to you, so let's have a look at one girl's experience.

Becky's Story

This summer I went on holiday with my friend and one evening at a pub we met two older guys. After talking for a while we went back to their place and ended up playing strip poker and getting off with them. I wanted to stop so I asked him to and he did. Then he said we could go up to his room and talk, so that his friend could stay with my friend. When we were there he started getting off with me again but said he wouldn't go any further. I wanted him to stop but he just kept telling me not to worry. I was too scared to really do anything and I was worried without knowing why.

He started getting very intimate and began fingering me and although I told him no, again he said not to worry. Before I really knew what was happening he was having sex with me. I was too scared to scream or anything and I just asked him to stop, but then I shut up and went along with it because I realized that nothing I did was going to make any difference.

I wasn't drunk and I don't think he was. I'm so confused. Was I raped or was I just stupid and easy? My friend said the same sort of thing had happened to her

and she's the only one I've told. I could never tell anyone else.

Becky

It's pretty obvious that what happened here had very little to do with love and everything to do with the animal passion of lust. But was it just another case of an older boy taking advantage of a younger girl? Well, there's no question that this did happen, but there were other forces at work which made it very easy for him to go from chatting her up in a crowded bar to having sex with her in a room far away from everyone else – all in the space of a couple of hours.

The first factor to take into account is hormones. Those chemical things that rush around your body making you feel fantastic one moment and in the depths of despair the next. Nature wants you to have sex and, because humans are at their most fertile in their teenage years, that's when Nature is at her trickiest working like a dynamo to push you into the arms of the opposite sex.

Sex – and lust – has a lot to do with excitement. You see your target (in Becky's case, the bloke in the pub) and your brain sends a message to your heart: 'Get ready for action.' Your pulse speeds up, you sit up straighter and become a hundred times more aware of that 'one' person. You move closer and as your eyes meet and you start chatting, you know that he/she is interested too. You feel high and buzzing as though the whole world is lit up.

Sounds wonderful? Yes – but it could describe

the greatest love affair on earth or a basic case of terminal lust. The catch is, at this stage you can't tell. Love involves caring, trust, responsibility and all those other boring things that your parents probably go on about, but most of all it means *knowing* the other person.

Becky didn't know this man but she was turned on both by him *and* by the feelings of excitement in her own mind and body so she projected her own romantic longings on to him – and ended up in a situation way out of control. (More about Becky in a moment.)

Do boys and girls fall in love in the same way?

Cynics have said that men give love in order to get sex while women offer sex in order to get love. Maybe that's true for some people but most of us want a mixture of things.

Deborah Tannen is a professor of linguistics (the study of language) who is famous for her research on the differences in the way men and women communicate. She thinks that we look at the world in different ways and that part of the reason we get so frustrated and confused in male/female relationships is because we don't understand how the minds of the opposite sex work. Women, she says, are driven by a need to get close to people, and they hate being isolated or lonely. They want emotional commitment, and the love part of their relationships will be vitally important.

But men, according to Deborah Tannen, see life in terms of their position in a kind of pecking order. They are always aware of where other people come in relation to themselves and they find it very uncomfortable to do or say anything that leaves them feeling one down. So rather than looking for intimacy and closeness they are struggling to get and keep the upper hand, if they can.

I can give you two very simple stereotypical examples of this. The first is the way in which men and women feel about asking for help. You're on your way to a party at a strange house. You walk or you drive up and down for some time unsuccessfully trying to find the right road. Most women would have no hesitation in stopping a passer-by and asking for directions. Men, on the other hand, tend to keep on tearing up and down streets looking and hoping to find the road where the party is. They don't want to ask for help because to do so is an admission of failure and it makes them feel vulnerable and uncomfortable.

Another example is the way that boys and girls (or men and women) cope with their emotional relationships. Girls talk about things. You see them together in corners in the classroom or the bar or club, talking and laughing about their hopes and fears and problems. If something goes wrong or they're worried about their relationship they confide in their friends. They talk about feelings. But boys often don't like talking about feelings at all. It feels wrong and uncomfortable to them and when you listen to their conversations you'll find they stick to facts on the whole. OK, some of the facts aren't exactly

accurate and a lot of boasting goes on, but that's down to the one-upmanship again. They certainly aren't comfortable with talking about doubts or worries or fears. Those sorts of words don't tend to come naturally to boys and though they may not be aware of it, they are probably scared

that their mates will think less of them if they stray into that kind of conversational territory.

So it's not surprising that one of the most common complaints in long-term relationships is from the woman saying that the man just doesn't talk to her. He won't share things with her. He, on the other hand, may be totally frustrated by her wish to witter on about anything and everything. Neither side is right or wrong – they're just different.

Misunderstandings

Going back to Becky and her situation, she was in a pub talking to an older guy who was definitely attractive. The old hormones get going and she finds herself feeling turned on and excited. He in his turn likes the look of her and makes an obvious effort to chat her up. Next comes the invitation to go back to his place. Becky sees this as a chance to get closer (emotionally as well as physically) and takes it as a sign that he likes her and wants to get to know her better. He, on the other hand, is definitely thinking of sex and, because he doesn't appreciate the difference between male and female thinking, assumes that because she goes home with him, she's prepared to go a lot further.

They get to the boys' rooms and strip poker is suggested. They've probably all had a fair bit to drink and it seems like a fun idea. The naughtiness of it is a turn-on (breaking taboos has always been sexy) but again, he assumes that because she agrees, she's game for anything and everything.

It's easy to argue that Becky should have known better than to go up to his bedroom with him. But she was enjoying the kissing and the stroking and assumed that she could trust him when he told her not to worry. In other words she interpreted 'Don't worry' as 'I won't do anything to hurt you.' He, however, saw the final green light when she went up to his room and he used the words 'Don't worry' to silence her objections. The fact that she did go silent made him think (wrongly) that she was happy with the situation and wanted to continue.

Quite possibly she was technically raped and I know from other things Becky told me that she was emotionally damaged and had to have a lot of help afterwards. But the fact remains that both she and this boy managed to get into this situation each thinking that what they were doing was OK. She was looking for emotional closeness, whilst he wanted sex; something he could boast about to his friends. A conquest for the night.

James's story shows some of the other side of the picture.

James's Story

At 17 all my mates had had strings of girlfriends and they were all (or so they said) sexually experienced. I got off with a couple of girls at school discos but I'd never been out with anyone and the only time a girl had asked me was when she was dared to by her friends.

My mates didn't go out of their way to make me feel bad but there was a lot of talk about sex and it was pretty obvious that I was the only one who hadn't done it. Then I met Lucy. She was new to the school and very quiet, but she always smiled at me. All my friends went on about her fancying me and kept saying I should ask her out. Eventually I did (though not in front of them) and was really surprised when she said yes. I'd only been out with her once when my friends started asking me how far I'd got. I didn't feel comfortable with that because I liked Lucy but they went on and on and kept saying that she must want it because she was obviously crazy about me.

I'm not proud of this bit, but after about a week I went round to her house when I knew her parents were going to be out, and we were kissing and snogging in her bedroom. I started to undress her and she said no, so I stopped and told her that it was all right. But then things got carried away again and I began fingering her. She didn't seem to mind so much and I couldn't contain myself so I started to have sex with her. The thing is, I really couldn't contain myself and I came before I could get inside her.

I felt very embarrassed but she was in tears. We cleaned ourselves up and had a cup of coffee, with her crying and sniffing all the time. Then I realized what I'd done. I'd nearly raped her. I felt awful. The next day my friends kept on asking me if I'd done it and then I felt awful with them. The next month was terrible. Lucy hardly spoke to me, or if she did she'd cry and my mates kept on pushing me to go round to her place and get on with it. I was almost relieved when eventually she said that she didn't want to go out with me but we could still be friends, although we've hardly spoken since.

James found himself stuck between the devil and the deep blue sea. His hormones and his male friends were all egging him on, pushing him to make a sexual conquest. Yet he obviously enjoyed the emotional closeness with Lucy and missed it when it ended. As in Becky's case they misread each other's signals and both ended up hurt.

SO HOW CAN YOU AVOID MISUNDERSTANDINGS?

There's no easy way, but the answer lies in being aware of the pressures and the differences between the sexes.

YOU CAN GET PUSHED INTO DOING THINGS FASTER THAN YOU MIGHT HAVE MEANT.	**1.** Sexual attraction is a powerful drug.
IT'S EASY TO MISINTERPRET EACH OTHER'S SIGNALS.	**2.** Boys and girls often look at things in different ways.
THINGS CAN QUICKLY GET OUT OF CONTROL AND YOU NEED TO PUT THE BRAKES ON SOONER RATHER THAN LATER.	**3.** Both of the above can drive a situation faster and faster.

Becky and Lucy both thought they were saying no, but the boys didn't hear it like that. They needed to say it earlier, more forcefully and more often, and most of all they needed to stand up and walk away from the situation to *show* that they weren't giving their consent to what was happening.

Hilary's Story

I was having a few friends round one night and one of them brought a lad with her who's a good friend of hers. He wanted to get off with me which my friend wasn't pleased about, but the rest of my friends said it was just jealousy and I shouldn't pay any attention. I took their advice and did. He was still going out with his girlfriend but said he'd tell her the next afternoon. Eventually he told her a week later. My friend said he'd do the same to me but everyone else thought she had personal interests and I should just ignore her.

After a couple of months he proposed to me. I was a bit wary but again my friends kept persuading me so I said yes. Six weeks later I phoned him as I'd been told he had something to tell me. He said he'd got off with someone else and that we should call everything off. I was gutted. I said it didn't matter, I would forgive him, but he said no, it was over.

I was devastated but my best friend was really comforting and she never once said, 'I told you so.' A couple of days later she told me that my ex had been seeing other people for most of the time we'd been engaged. That made everything a lot worse.

I know I should never have got involved with him because of what she'd told me. She'd warned me of his reputation of using girls but all my other friends said that he'd changed since he'd been with me and I suppose I wanted to believe them more than her.

It took me a lot of courage to write this for you and hopefully it shows that you can't trust everyone and that it's usually the people closest to you who know best.

Hilary wanted a boyfriend. She wanted someone to be close to and share things with. Her best friend told her this wasn't an ideal guy but he seemed too good to ignore. When the rest of her mates started persuading her to go for it she was ready to believe that her best friend was only motivated by jealousy. Hilary had a bad time but at least she got out of it fairly quickly. And she managed to keep her friend.

Her story illustrates another two points that are worth adding to 1, 2 and 3 above:

REMEMBER, A GOOD RELATIONSHIP WILL WAIT BUT GOING TOO FAST CAN LEAD YOU INTO SOMETHING YOU'RE NOT READY FOR.	**4.** **If in doubt or feeling wary, HOLD BACK.**
IF SOMEONE REALLY CARES FOR YOU (YOUR MUM, BROTHER OR BEST FRIEND ETC) THEN AT LEAST LISTEN TO WHAT THEY HAVE TO SAY ABOUT YOUR BOYFRIEND OR GIRLFRIEND. MAYBE IT ISN'T WHAT YOU WANT TO HEAR BUT THEY ARE MORE LIKELY TO TELL YOU THE TRUTH THAN A GANG IF MATES WHO COULD BE OUT TO STIR THINGS UP.	**5.** **If you trust someone, you should trust their opinions.**

MISTAKING LONELINESS FOR LOVE

Most women want to be close to someone and they see relationships as a way to obtain that closeness. Because of this they can sometimes fool themselves into thinking they're in love when all they're really doing is running away from loneliness.

Pam's Story
I'd been going out with this man for sixteen months. It was a very on/off relationship and he was never quite sure who or what he wanted but he always came back

to me. Throughout the whole time he was continually asking me to marry him and have his baby. In the end I felt he loved me so agreed to marry him.

It was to be a second marriage for both of us and he wanted it to happen as soon as possible, so we arranged everything in a week and were married by special licence.

As soon as we came out of the register office I was very quiet and I kept thinking, 'What on earth have I done?' On the one hand I wanted to go through with it but on the other I wondered what the hell I was doing. It was too late to put a stop to it though. The ball was rolling and I somehow felt I had to carry on. He had arranged everything, witnesses, flowers and even cooked and made all the food for a few friends afterwards.

We were married at the end of February and he left me two weeks later for another woman who claimed to be pregnant by him. I haven't seen him from that day to this. I guess in the long run I pushed myself into this relationship because I didn't want to be on my own, even though my 'inner self' was telling me that it would be wrong.

Pam, aged 27

Susan's Story

I was 20 and a few months previously I'd split from the boyfriend that I truly loved. Feeling lonely I advertised in the Lonely Hearts column of our local paper and this is how I came to meet John. On our first date we went for a drink in the pub and then a walk along the beach, where he told me he loved me. Upset from the break with my ex, I was convinced that after only a couple of hours I loved him too. Two days later he proposed and two months later we became engaged. From the minute we were engaged that was it, I knew I'd made a mistake. But everything was happening too fast. I felt we'd made a public declaration to get married and that's what we should do. Both my sisters had had broken engagements and I can still remember my parents' reactions.

I suppose my ending up married was a combination of my parents and family, my friends who were excited and my own stupidity. I was caught up in the romance of it all. Although we were married in a register office there was still the excitement of choosing a dress, the flowers and the rings and I was at the centre of it all.

Our marriage lasted eight days short of the year. He got a job in another part of the country and I think I was so relieved he'd gone that I waited two months and then asked for a divorce. He agreed and then disappeared.

Susan, aged 23

It's interesting that both Pam and Susan knew they were making a mistake before they got married. Yet they talk about a ball being set rolling and how difficult it is to stop something when everyone else is expecting it to happen. It's so easy to live our lives for other people's expectations. Both these women knew that they were getting into a relationship that wasn't right for them but they still went through with it. They both ended up hurt, although at least it was over relatively quickly.

77

If I'd had a chance to advise them before the wedding I'd have told them to wait. ***Whenever you aren't sure, you should hold back.*** I would also have suggested that they examine their own motives to see how big a part loneliness played in the wish to get married. I suspect that if they had had a chance to expand their lives, make some more friends and generally raise their own self-confidence, while they may still have been looking for a long-term relationship they wouldn't have fallen into this kind of marriage so quickly.

Feeling good, or simply better, about yourself helps protect you from the dangers of loneliness. Feeling lonely isn't just about being on your own or apart from other people; it's a sensation of neglect and isolation. When we say we're lonely what we're

really looking for is a spot of tender loving care or cherishing. Sometimes we're lucky enough to find someone to provide this fairly easily but, as we've seen above, there can be drawbacks to the quick fix. Loneliness can easily blur your judgement, so it's worth trying to make yourself feel better first. Provide your own cherishing and TLC. Spoil yourself. It needn't be expensive – just give yourself some time and space for simple, enjoyable things that make you feel good. You'll feel the loneliness retreating and you'll be in a much stronger position to make new friends and relationships.

PAYING THE DEBT

Sometimes, when we're lonely, we do find other people who offer the love and support we need to flourish. It's a wonderful sensation, like discovering an oasis in the desert, and it's not surprising that we feel a great warmth and gratitude and relief towards them. But it's easy to mistake that for love, and sometimes the strength of that gratitude can pull you in to a relationship that isn't appropriate for you. You're paying the debt, but at great cost to yourself.

Beth's Story
When I was 16 I was best friends with a girl who happened to be a lesbian. I was the only one she had told and I was able to be a support to her. She helped me a lot as well because I was shy and had problems at home. This meant that I found it difficult to become close friends with anybody. I had lots of acquaintances

but Sheila was my only true mate. I didn't mind that she was gay and she didn't mind that I sometimes shut her out as she knew I would eventually come back and confide in her. I'd never had anyone to trust and tell secrets to before and I probably wasn't that good at being a 'best' friend.

In the summer I went away on holiday with Sheila and her parents. On the last night we sat up talking and she began to cry, telling me how difficult it was and how she was trying to pluck up the courage to tell her parents about her sexuality. I comforted her for a while, holding her and telling her everything would be OK, when she suddenly turned to me and said, 'I love you.' I replied that I loved her too because I did, particularly as she had been the first person to show me any real affection.

Before I knew what was happening she was kissing me. I didn't know what to do. I hadn't even kissed a boy before, never mind a girl. A series of thoughts flashed through my mind. I knew that I loved Sheila and I suppose I had become dependent on her friendship. I couldn't imagine life without her, but the main thought in my head was that I couldn't hurt her.

So to protect her feelings I began to kiss her back. I didn't want it at all and I knew it was wrong but I couldn't think of what else I could do. The next morning we hardly spoke at breakfast or on the coach home. I think she was really pleased but I was inwardly kicking myself and thinking what on earth to do.

I realized that whatever I did I would hurt this person who had helped me so much. It was an impossible situation. It's hard to believe now but it carried on for just over three months. We hugged and kissed and every time we did it I told her that I loved her. I hated myself so much. It seemed like she'd placed all her trust in me and I was lying to her. The longer it went on the worse it became, but I couldn't tell her it was over. There was no way I could win.

By the end I was weary. I knew I had to do it and I arranged to meet her in town and we sat on a bench while I said, 'Sheila, I can't see you any more.' She quietly asked why and I said, 'I love you, I do, but I'm not in love with you.' I was crying but she was very calm about it. Basically we tried to be friends again but it couldn't be the same. We ended up arguing all the time and now we don't talk any more.

It was the worst three months of my life because I knew all the time that I was straight, but I kept telling myself I might learn to love her the way she wanted, but I don't think I ever believed it myself.

Beth

Beth and Sheila had an intense friendship and eventually Sheila tentatively asked if they could take it further. Beth was confused because although she knew she was straight she felt she owed Sheila a debt and wanted to make her happy. The fact that this was a lesbian relationship is irrelevant; it could easily have happened with a man and a woman. The point is that Beth found herself trying to act out a feeling that she didn't truly believe. She was doing it to avoid hurting her much-valued friend, but, all the same, she ended up hurting her friend a great deal. As Beth says, it was a no-win situation.

The only way their friendship could have survived was for Beth to have been honest right from the start. Even if she hadn't felt strong enough to say no, she could have asked for time to think it over. It's that golden rule again: *Whenever you aren't sure, you should hold back.* Remember, a good relationship will wait for you, but going too fast will lead you to something you're not ready for.

Chapter Four

But if You Really Loved Me . . .
DECIDING FOR YOURSELF HOW FAR
YOU WANT TO GO

Have you ever felt that things were moving too fast?
And have you ever been scared to say 'stop' in case
you upset your boyfriend/girlfriend?

I'm a 15-year-old girl and my best friend has a brother
of 17. I really like him and have done for a long time. My
friend passes messages to me about him. Sometimes I
see him on my own after school. I'm not going out with
him but he asks me to do sexual things with him. I'm
frightened he would tell people if I did these things or
that he might hate me if I don't. What should I do?
   Tanya

I've been going out with this lad for only about two
weeks and he already wants me to go further with him,
e.g. fingering, blow-jobs etc. I'm only 13 and not ready
to go further with him. But if I don't he will probably
dump me and I really like him. What shall I do?
   Diana

I had a serious boyfriend from when I was 15 to when I was 17. He was the one who broke it up and I felt very lonely after that. It took about a year before I felt able to go out with anyone and when Dan asked me to a party I was thrilled. We had a great evening but later he drove me home and somehow we ended up at his place.

When he asked me in I kind of knew what he meant, but I thought I'd just go in, have a quick drink and then go home. He didn't see it that way. I couldn't get him off me and when I said I wasn't prepared to sleep with him so quickly he got angry. He said we'd known each other for ages (which was true) and if I wasn't prepared for this then why had I gone out with him? I didn't know what to say. I only knew that the more he pushed me, the less I felt like going to bed with him.

Caroline, aged 19

Letters like these make up a big part of my agony postbag at *Mizz*. Girls, and not just 13- or 14-year-olds, often feel under pressure from their boyfriends to get into a sexual relationship much faster than they would really like. The crunch usually comes when the boy utters the immortal words, 'But if you really loved me . . .' This is a very effective line as it doesn't take much imagination on the girl's part to hear the unspoken threat that if she doesn't deliver she can kiss him goodbye.

Of course lots of couples start having sex without these problems. They both want it, it's a joint decision and they take care of each other by organizing effective contraception and protection. That's fine, but I find it profoundly depressing that so many girls still feel under threat to do something that they just aren't ready for.

Is it always the girl who's the victim?

It is usually boys who try it on with girls, but it certainly does happen the other way around. I probably don't hear so much about it because most boys don't put up a fight, but sometimes blokes aren't so sure they want to get into the full sexual thing.

I'm 16 and have been going out with my boyfriend for two years. The problem is that we love each other but have gone no further than simply getting off. I feel ready for a sexual relationship but I don't think he feels the same way. We spend lots of time together but sex is never mentioned. Should I speak to him about it? Do you think there is anything I can say or do to get our relationship moving further?

Four months ago I broke off with him as I was tempted to go with another bloke, but after two weeks

I realized how much I loved and missed him and we got back together. I feel now that the split was because things were coming to a standstill. I value his personality and am NOT using him for sex, but I'm going to go crazy if we don't take things further.
Pia

Pia isn't putting undue pressure on her boyfriend but I'm sure she's making it clear that she'd like things to move a bit faster. She recently broke up with him because she fancied someone else and that must have focused his thoughts on what was really going on between them. Yet here they are, going out for two years but not feeling able to talk about sex. Pia's desperate but she needs to get a bit closer to him before she can have her wicked way with him. For a start she needs to tell him how she feels and give him a chance to say how he wants things to go. She needs to realize that some boys are dead scared of pressure.

David's Story

I'd been going out with Mel for nearly eight months and I guess I really liked her. She was 17 and I was two years older, and she knew that I had slept with a couple of previous girlfriends and often used to ask about them. We did a lot with each other and a couple of times managed to spend the night in bed together, but we never went all the way. Gradually she started making comments and saying that she'd really like to do it. I knew it would be the first time for her but it scared me because I also knew she would see it as a major commitment. I tried explaining this and saying that I wasn't ready for anything heavy and she kept saying it was all right, it was all right. Then one weekend we'd been to a party, came back to my place and things just happened.

I used a condom although she didn't say anything about it at all, but I knew as soon as it was over that it had been a big mistake. She just lay there holding me and telling me how much it meant and the next thing I knew she was going on about plans for our future. It was like she'd grabbed me and I was going to be shackled to her for the rest of my life. The next couple of weeks were awful and I felt I was suffocating in all her plans and talk of the future. I remember I tried telling her that things hadn't changed but she looked at me as though I was mad and said that of course they had and now we *really* loved each other.

I knew then that I couldn't let it go on and the next day I told her it was over. It was terrible and I know I broke her heart, but I just couldn't stay and become part of her fantasy.

David, aged 20

David knew that his girlfriend saw having sex as a major commitment and held back from it because he was not prepared to make that commitment. When they did sleep together his fears were proved true. His girlfriend thought that making love had the same meaning for him as it did for her. The result was one pressurized, terrified boyfriend – who quickly did a runner.

DIFFERENT ATTITUDES TO SEX

Boys and girls both enjoy sex; it's designed to be a pleasurable activity, and particularly during your teenage years, your hormones are rushing around in your blood, making the idea of sex incredibly attractive. But there is still a sex difference in the way we approach it.

Girls generally do equate sex with love. To them it is literally 'making love', and intercourse is the closest form of affection they can achieve. If a girl's boyfriend doesn't find it very easy to say complimentary things or talk about his feelings (and let's face it, lots of boys don't) then she's more likely to crave the emotional closeness that comes with sex. In other words, she enjoys the sex but she also gets a buzz out of the feelings of love that go with it.

For most boys things are slightly different. They have just as strong a sex drive, but in many cases it isn't complicated by feelings of love. Sex is seen as an exciting adventure and no possible chance should be turned down. I asked a group of boys how they saw this difference.

'Girls are always giggling and cuddling up to each other. They spend loads of time talking about boyfriends, but I think boys are more likely to talk about football, then going out and drinking, and then girls – and what we do with them.'

'Girls seem to talk about sex and things amongst themselves much more than boys do. With us it becomes a laugh whereas with girls they actually discuss what happens and what they feel.'

'Men find it much harder to talk about emotions – I don't know why, but it's probably to do with being macho.'

'We all know what each other does and if a bloke has it off at the weekend we'd probably write up something like "Well done, John" on the blackboard on Monday morning. There's no way he's going to keep it secret. After all, it's good, isn't it? And the girl? Well, she must be a slag, mustn't she?'

'Boys are expected to have sex, aren't they? Even my dad goes on about it, saying how many girls he'd slept with by the time he was my age. Mind you, it's different for my sister!'

89

'Some blokes talk a load of bull when it comes to sex. So you know to downgrade everything they say. But you still listen all the same.'

How can sex ruin a relationship?

David's letter earlier summed it all up: he said that after he had slept with his girlfriend, she felt there had been an immense emotional commitment made, whereas he just felt scared. People can sometimes make vast assumptions about their relationship once they've been to bed with their partners, and the very intensity of their feelings can be terrifying. It's not that they necessarily start talking about playing happy families; often they feel worried that this new stage in their relationship leaves them too vulnerable. They are scared their boyfriend or girlfriend will leave, so they start looking and asking for reassurance.

But not everyone feels comfortable with emotional intimacy and sometimes girls cope with it better than boys. Knowing that they can't necessarily deliver the commitment and reassurance their girlfriend seeks, boys can feel threatened and are likely to turn and run. Sex effectively puts an end to their relationship.

So how do I know if I'm ready?

The general answer to that is if you aren't sure whether you're ready or not to have sex then it's probably best to wait for a bit longer. Feeling under pressure because everyone else is doing it or, even worse, because your partner says or implies that they'll run off and leave you if you don't deliver, is *never* a good enough reason for going ahead. Sex is an important and exciting part of life and it should always be *your* choice whether you do it – not someone else's.

Sex should also be something that you have some degree of control over. Too many girls write to me and say that they went to a party, had something to drink and 'one thing led to another'. Drinking alcohol and taking drugs loosens your inhibitions, and you are more likely to find yourself doing things outside your normal behaviour, but the after-effects still hurt.

Marianne's story shows how she lost her virginity and how she feels about it now . . .

Marianne's Story

It all started at Easter when we were staying in our caravan near a country club place. My two friends and I all went to the pool room to check out the talent. It was a Sunday, so it was the most popular day of the week and there were a lot of people there. We were casually glancing around when I noticed one guy staring at me. He started smiling so I smiled back a bit, but he then left with his friends. Over the next week of my holiday I saw him a couple of times, but nothing developed. But I knew already that I would like to go out with him.

In May that year my cousin got married and as I was walking through the church to sit down I noticed the same boy sitting across the aisle from me. At the reception I got talking to him and throughout the whole day we stuck together. I found out that he worked with my cousin's new husband. He'd left school when he was 16 and he already had a girlfriend although she wasn't coming to the wedding. I'd had a lot to drink, so when he asked me to dance to the slow songs I jumped at the chance. I'd already arranged to stay at my friend's house that night so eventually my parents went home and I stayed at the reception.

This boy (I'll call him John) called me over to him and when he kissed me it was everything I ever dreamt it would be. He then took my hand and led me outside.

After we had kissed for a while I felt him fingering me off, but I was so drunk I couldn't tell him to stop. The next thing I remember was him asking me to pull him off and I kept saying no. I was only 15 and I wasn't very experienced when it came to boys. We kissed on for another while and then I felt him put his penis inside me, but I thought we couldn't be having sex because we were standing up. He kept on pushing himself up inside me and I kept on saying no and pushing him away, but he was very strong.

Eventually I succeeded and ran away. I was in tears and I cried my eyes out to my friend. She told me to come back inside because if I stayed away he would know that he'd hurt me. I went in and walked straight past him. He called me back to talk to him and I couldn't believe he was acting as though nothing had happened. His mates seemed really dead-on and I enjoyed myself chatting to them until one guy asked me how far I had gone with John and what number was I on his list. Listening to this I realized he had a record of trying it on with girls.

At around 2 a.m. my friend's parents told us they were going, so John said he would walk me out. On our way a couple of other people I knew said to me to be very careful with him and I can remember thinking that I wished they'd said that earlier.

I didn't see John again until three months later when I went to my first over-age disco. I plucked up the courage to go over and talk to him, and he started buying me drinks and managed to get me drunk. We went outside to his car. One thing led to another and we had sex.

And today? Well, I wish I'd never met John. He really made me feel cheap and dirty. In a way I'm glad it did happen because everyone loses their virginity sometime, but at the same time I regret it because I was saving myself for someone I really loved and my feelings for John now are hate. I still see him, although the only contact we have is to wave to each other.

Marianne feels hurt and used because she lost all control of the situation. Yet, despite the fact that she was effectively assaulted if not raped by John at their first meeting, she voluntarily started chatting to him again at the disco and ended up having sex a second time. Sometimes it can be very hard to distinguish between different emotions. Marianne was attracted to him but didn't like what he did to her. She knew he was using her but, while in some ways it scared her, she also liked the feeling and, at the time, got all the sex stuff confused with love and affection. It was only later when she looked back at what had happened with a slightly colder eye that she felt so bad about events.

Marianne's story isn't unusual and I hope she doesn't feel too guilty or bitter about what happened. She knows now that sex isn't the same as love, and with luck, she'll wait a bit longer before going so far with her next boyfriend. And more to the point, I hope she'll make sure her next boyfriend really is a boyfriend, rather than someone who fancies his chances with a half-drunk girl.

UNDER PRESSURE

So if you're feeling pressurized, and you're not sure you want to go further, what should you do?

Step 1: Slow things down.
It's very corny old agony aunt advice but it's still true that if a boy threatens to leave you if you don't have

sex with him, then the chances are he'll leave you even if you do. It's probable that his main objective is to have sex and gain sexual experience. He sees you as a means to an end, and not as a person he's in love with. So if you experience direct emotional blackmail just think of a giant neon sign flashing NO on top of his head. He isn't worth it.

If your relationship is moving towards sex and you aren't sure how far you want to take it or how fast you want to go, then it's time to apply some brakes. If you're under 16 you have a ready-made excuse in the legal age of consent. Your boyfriend may not be very impressed by this, but point out that he could face criminal charges if he goes ahead and has sex with you. The bigger the age difference between you (if there is one) then the worse it would be for him, and if you are very young he could even face a life sentence. For more information on this, see chapter nine, 'Rights and Wrongs'.

Step 2: Talk about sex.

If you are trying to avoid being pushed into having sex, mentioning the subject at all may seem a crazy idea but it's important to give your partner a chance to learn how you feel and what it is that's worrying you. Sometimes talking helps you sort out your own feelings better too. Remember, if someone cares for you they will be prepared to wait a bit longer, and they'll certainly want to show they care by making sure that contraception and protection are sorted out in advance. In fact this is a brilliant and sneaky test for any bloke you suspect may be out for sex rather than love. It's amazing how many boys make all kinds of excuses to wriggle out of the responsibility of contraception – either because they don't want to show their ignorance or because they just can't be bothered.

I'm going steady with a boy and last weekend we were in his bedroom and we ended up on the bed. We would have gone all the way if I hadn't said I had my monthly period. I'm very worried about contraception and I overheard him talking to his best mate saying that we were going to have sex and that we didn't need to use any contraception. I don't know what to do. I'm scared to say anything about contraception, but I don't want to end up pregnant. I want to have sex with him, but not without a condom. I don't know what to do.
Olive, aged 16

Would you be too embarrassed to talk about contraception? Do you think that 'getting technical' spoils the romance between two people? I don't know where Olive's boyfriend gets his ideas from but maybe, like many other people, he thinks pregnancy is something that simply doesn't have to worry him. My guess is that he doesn't know much about contraception and he's certainly too embarrassed to find out from anyone, so instead he brags that he doesn't need it and he'll just do what he wants anyway.

Olive presumably likes this boy and says she does want to have sex with him but, given his attitude, I don't think it's going to be a very happy or long-lived relationship.

Jenny has an even worse story to tell.

I've been going out with my boyfriend for just over two months, and over the past few weeks we've begun having sex. Every time we've done it I've made him use a condom, but the problem is he hates using them. A few of his close mates have told him that it's not fair on him for me to choose what type of contraception we should use, as it should be a joint decision. He's told me that if I do it without a condom he'll pull out before he comes, but I don't want to do this as I know that sperm is released before a boy ejaculates.

Some of my friends have said I should do it without one in my safe period, but as my boyfriend has had sex with at least one other girl before me and didn't use a condom, I'm worried about catching a disease. Other friends have suggested that I should go on the pill but I'm worried about my mum finding out and the side-effects of the pill.

My boyfriend makes using condoms difficult as I always have to buy them. I would get them free from the Family Planning Clinic but my boyfriend doesn't like the kind they give away. I know that you'll tell me to stick to my guns and make him use one, but it's getting really difficult now and I often feel guilty for making him use condoms.

Jenny, aged 16

As you can imagine, words just about failed me when I read Jenny's letter. Not only does her boyfriend make her go and buy her own condoms (they could at least share the cost) but he then whinges about the type she gets. Luckily Jenny knows that it isn't safe to rely on a 'safe' period without a lot of help from a doctor or Family Planning nurse and, more to the point, using such a method or taking the pill wouldn't give her protection against sexually transmitted diseases or HIV.

She's prepared to have sex with him but she wants to do it safely. All he's doing is causing trouble and offering half-baked myths about keeping her safe by pulling out in time. This simply doesn't work. Apart from it being very difficult for a bloke to withdraw his penis just at the moment when his whole body is telling him to keep it in there, you also get a drop or two of semen at the end of the penis a few seconds or even minutes before ejaculation. One drop can contain three million sperm, which gives you a fair chance of getting pregnant almost before you've got anywhere.

Reading Jenny's letter made me want to grab a condom and stick it over her idiot boyfriend's head. She probably wouldn't agree with me, but I think she'd be better off without him. All he causes her is trouble and hassle – yet she ends up feeling guilty for asking him to behave responsibly.

Step 3: If you're still in doubt, say no.
Remember sex should be *your* choice. Nobody has a right to push you into it, and however much they might be expecting it (or you may feel you owe it to them), that still doesn't mean you have to do it.

But saying no to someone you're fond of is never easy. You're scared of upsetting them or, even worse, losing them, and even if you're not exactly prepared to do what they want, it's sometimes very tempting to sit on the fence and keep them hoping that you may come round to their way of thinking.

Karen's Story
I go to an all-girls school and didn't have a boyfriend until I was 15. I met Jeremy at a school disco when a whole gang of boys came from another school in town. I've always been quite shy so I found it very hard to talk to him at first, but he was also fairly quiet. Somehow

that made it easier. At first we didn't really go out anywhere, we'd just meet sometimes after school, and he'd ring me a few times a week. My mum teased me about him quite a lot and kept saying I should invite him home sometime. Gradually he started coming over and my mum and dad really liked him.

Things progressed and by the time it was about two months before my 16th birthday we were doing pretty much everything apart from intercourse. One evening when we were in my bedroom he said that he'd really like to do it. I suppose I'd been expecting it for a while but I knew I wasn't ready. He must have seen the look on my face because then he said it didn't matter and he'd wait until I was 16.

I spent the next two months dreading my birthday. I felt that as soon as I was 16 he would expect me to sleep with him, and although I loved him I just didn't feel ready for that. It was something about him expecting it too much, and also I didn't fancy the idea of doing it at home while my parents were in the house. My mum had always said that I could talk to her about sex and get advice if I was going to start a relationship, but I just didn't feel comfortable with it, and I thought I'd be letting her down to sleep with him in those circumstances.

On my 16th birthday he took me out for a meal, and when we got back he gave me an extra present – it was a pack of condoms all wrapped up in pretty paper. I probably looked very embarrassed. I laughed a bit and then told him it wasn't the right time of the month. He looked disappointed but said something about not expecting it straight away, and we carried on for another couple of weeks not really talking about it. But all the time I knew he was thinking about it and expecting me to do it.

Finally he asked me again and at first I said OK, and then changed my mind when I could hear my mum moving around downstairs. I told him I wouldn't do it until we could be alone. Three weeks later his parents went away for the weekend. I went round to his place and it was obvious what he was expecting, but I knew as soon as we started kissing and hugging on his bed that I couldn't do it.

It was awful. He called me terrible names and said that I was a tease and had led him on. I couldn't bear it and ended up locking myself in the bathroom for ages. Everything we'd had had been so good, but because of sex (or rather me not wanting it) it had all gone rotten and we were just screaming at each other.

Karen

What would you have done in Karen's situation? Would you have felt able to tell your boyfriend you didn't want sex yet? Karen loved her boyfriend and didn't want to upset him, so she didn't feel able to be honest about her own wishes. She knew she wasn't ready to have sex, but she was scared to say it in case he went off her. The result, as you can see, was disastrous.

There's no easy way out of this situation, but it might have been an idea for Karen to have been more honest earlier on. She could have said that she didn't feel ready for sex, and one of the reasons that she was so unsure was the feeling that she was being pressurized by her boyfriend. Saying 'I need more time to decide and I can't do it while I'm under pressure' isn't so very difficult. Putting it like that makes it very plain that your partner needs to back off for a bit to give you time to sort things out.

If you're under pressure, but don't want to go further

DON'T GIVE IN TO EMOTIONAL BLACKMAIL. REMEMBER THAT IF SOMEONE REALLY LOVES YOU THEY'LL BE PREPARED TO WAIT UNTIL YOU ARE SURE YOU ARE READY.

1.
Slow things down.

CHECK OUT WHAT YOUR PARTNER THINKS ABOUT CONTRACEPTION AND PROTECTION. THEIR ATTITUDE CAN GIVE YOU A GOOD IDEA OF HOW MUCH THEY ARE REALLY CONCERNED FOR YOU — AS OPPOSED TO JUST WANTING SEX.

2.
Talk about sex.

SEX SHOULD ALWAYS BE YOUR CHOICE AND NOBODY HAS THE RIGHT TO PUSH YOU INTO IT.

3.
If you're still in doubt, say no.

Chapter Five

I Never Thought it Could Happen to Me
COPING WITH UNPLANNED PREGNANCY

Every year in the UK over 8,000 girls under the age of 16 get pregnant. And nearly every one of them thought it could never happen to them.

WHAT GOES WRONG?

Why do so many girls get pregnant? Some girls get pregnant the first and the only time they have sex. Perhaps they had faith in the myth that you can't get pregnant the first time you do it (believe me, it is a myth) or maybe they weren't expecting the relationship to go so far so quickly. Certainly a lot of people think that doing it once or twice without precautions won't make any difference. But they hadn't reckoned on Mother Nature. Teenage girls are at the most fertile time of their lives and a 16-year-old having unprotected sex roughly halfway between her menstrual periods (i.e. during her fertile period) has an approximately 70% chance of getting pregnant the first time she has sex. That's pretty mind-blowing.

Other girls get 'carried away' and find themselves having sex without any precautions because things get out of control. The typical part of the letters I read goes something like: 'We went to a party, had a couple of drinks and one thing led to another . . .' Unfortunately one thing very often does lead to another – and the end result is usually a lot of unhappiness.

Some girls believe their boyfriends when they say that everything will be OK. Boys don't exactly mean to lie but, as a breed, they hate losing face so are unlikely to admit their ignorance of anything. If their mates have told them the first time is always safe or pulling their penis out quickly stops the girl getting pregnant, then they tend to believe them. Unfortunately, because you love them and because they say it with such authority you're likely to believe them too. That's when the trouble starts.

For most girls, because their menstrual cycles and times of ovulation (that's when the egg is released) can vary, there is no reliable 'safe' period to have sex. And having sex without contraception leads, in most cases, sooner or later to pregnancy.

In some cases, contraception is used, but it fails at the critical moment. Condoms are a really good method but sometimes they do split. It is important to put them on properly and to avoid snagging them with sharp or ragged nails, but even then I know some people do find them very hard to use. The pill is another good method, but if you get sick or have diarrhoea soon after taking it, or you get drunk and throw up at a party, it's not going to work very well. Some antibiotics interfere with its effectiveness too, so it's a good idea to remind your doctor that you're taking the pill if he prescribes anything for you.

Whatever the reason, the important thing is not how you got pregnant, but what you do next.

Too many girls bury their heads in the sand. They know there's a chance they may be pregnant, but they're too scared even to sit down and work out when their last period was. They don't want to face the possibility and they certainly don't want anyone else to know. It's as though pretending it isn't happening will make it go away. Unfortunately that doesn't work.

When I was researching a previous book I spoke to a doctor who had worked in the casualty department of my local hospital. He told me the heart-rending story of a young girl who was brought in by her mother with severe abdominal pains. The mother thought she had appendicitis or an ulcer or something, but it was very obvious that the girl was in labour. She was put in a cubicle on a bed with a curtain separating her from the chair on which her mother sat. Her contractions got greater and more painful and she was biting her lips trying not to scream, but she kept saying to the doctor, 'Please don't tell my mum what's happening.' Eventually the baby was born and the girl still didn't want her mum to know. The amazing thing was that the mother on the other side of the curtains listened to her daughter in pain and then heard the crying of the baby, but was still able to pretend that none of it was happening to her or her daughter. Parents can be pretty good at sticking their heads in the sand too!

Dani was 16 and over four months pregnant when she wrote to me.

I went to the doctor for a pregnancy test when I was over a month late for my period but I never went back for the results. I told my boyfriend about it and he doesn't seem to mind, but I just can't tell my parents. It's not that they're strict but they're always going on about young girls getting pregnant and how the parents are to blame. I just don't know what to do. My parents don't even know that I have a boyfriend so this is making matters worse. My dad will go absolutely mad if I tell him, not only with me but with my boyfriend, so please don't tell me to tell my parents. I was also wondering if it's too late to have an abortion?

Dani was out of luck because by the time I got her letter it almost certainly was too late for her to arrange an abortion (more about this later and in chapter nine, 'Rights and Wrongs'). She had taken far too long to get to grips with her situation, but more to the point she had run a great risk by cutting herself off from medical and counselling help during her pregnancy. It's a common mistake to think that you only go to the doctor when you are ready to decide whether to keep the baby or have an abortion. However, though most pregnancies are uncomplicated, there are occasions when things go wrong.

That's why it's so vital that you see a doctor or at least go to a Family Planning or youth advisory clinic *as soon as you think you may be pregnant*. It's easy to be like Dani and leave it for another day, and then another week but, no matter how you feel about having a baby, you could be putting your own life in danger.

Carrie was 16 and had had sex with a couple of boys without using a condom or anything else. She never worried about the possibility that she could be pregnant until disaster struck.

Carrie's Story

I'd gone out with a friend drinking on a Monday night and then spent the night at her house, so Mum wouldn't find out that I'd been under-age drinking at night clubs. The next morning I felt sick and put it down to a bad hangover. Then I stood up and collapsed. I just managed to get home but still felt awful. I spent that night in pure pain. The following morning I went to the doctor who had me rushed into hospital.

The reason was that I had become pregnant and the foetus was stuck in my left fallopian tube and another 24 hours would have killed me. I had an emergency operation and had to stay in hospital for a week, but thankfully I'm fine now. Obviously my mum had to find out and luckily she's been great about it. We haven't told anyone else.

The whole thing has left me with a lot of pain and I'm a bit scared to have sex, even with contraception. I guess what I'm saying is that you shouldn't have sex without using a condom or something, it's just not worth the pain that I've been through.

What happened to Carrie is called an ectopic pregnancy. It is when a fertilized egg gets stuck in one of the tubes on its way to the uterus. It starts to grow within a very small space and quickly causes pain and swelling and eventually internal bleeding. It's very dangerous and extremely painful and Carrie is very lucky to be alive. If she had been keeping track of her periods and had suspected she was pregnant she might have seen a doctor, or visited a clinic where they would have checked that the growing foetus wasn't stuck in her fallopian tubes.

When it comes to pregnancy, ignoring the problem does not make it go away. Sticking your head in the sand doesn't work. However you got into the situation, what you now have to do is take control.

WHAT TO DO IF YOU THINK YOU MIGHT BE PREGNANT

Step 1: It may not be too late to use contraception!

If you find yourself having unprotected sex or something goes wrong with your contraception at the crucial time then you don't have to wait biting your nails to see if your next period is late.

Up to 3 days

Emergency contraception (it used to be called the 'morning-after pill') is available from GPs, Family Planning Clinics, Brook Advisory Centres, and possibly soon over the counter in pharmacies. It can be used up to three days (72 hours) after unprotected sex. It's basically a large dose of the same hormones found in the contraceptive pill which, if taken within the 72 hours, stops a fertilized egg implanting itself in your uterus and developing into a baby.

Up to 5 days
If you're too late for the emergency contraceptive pill it's possible you may be able to have an IUD fitted up to 5 days after unprotected sex, although this isn't always advisable for young women. If you need advice on this, contact your GP or a Family Planning Clinic or a Brook Advisory Centre and ask for an *urgent* appointment for *emergency contraception*. Some GPs and clinics operate drop-in surgeries, in which case you should go and wait for an appointment. Remember you only have a very short time to get this sorted out.

After 5 days
Emergency contraception is only available up until 5 days after intercourse. After that your next priority is to find out whether or not you are pregnant.

Step 2: Find out if you really are pregnant.
The first sign of pregnancy is usually a late or missed period. But of course if you don't keep records of your periods, or if they're very irregular anyway, you won't be able to use this as a warning sign. There are many other symptoms of pregnancy but they vary from person to person and a lot of them don't start until later. However many people do find that they start feeling very tired and go off certain foods or alcohol or cigarettes almost immediately they conceive. But sometimes it's possible to convince yourself you're pregnant when you're not.

I'm a 16-year-old girl and I've been secretly seeing a 20-year-old lad for about eight months. We have a great relationship and I love him very much. We've had sex twice and both times we used a condom. My periods are usually very regular but since having sex with him I am two weeks late. Is there any chance that I could be pregnant even though we used a condom? My stomach is swollen and my breasts are enlarged. Are these signs of pregnancy? I've had a bit of discharge but not as much as usual. I haven't eaten properly for about two months so could that have anything to do with my period being late?

Melanie

If Melanie and her boyfriend used a condom properly on both occasions then the chances are that she isn't pregnant. Anxiety and worry (and she's certainly worried) can often delay a period, and sudden changes in eating habits or loss or gain of weight can also stop menstruation temporarily. We all tend to feel a bit swollen and often have sore breasts before our periods start, and if a period is delayed by a week or two then these pre-menstrual symptoms can get even worse. So all of Melanie's symptoms could be due to things other than pregnancy, but she won't know whether or not she's pregnant until she has a test. And in the meantime she'll continue to worry.

Pregnancy tests can be done from the first day your period is due. You can buy DIY kits from the pharmacist, although they can be quite expensive. If

you're going to get one, make sure you look for the kind that offers you a result in a few minutes and that doesn't have to be done first thing in the morning. That way you can do it in privacy in your own time rather than with the whole family banging on the bathroom door. You can also take a sample of urine in a clean bottle or jam jar into the chemist who will do a test for you. Again you have to pay for this.

It's probably a better idea to see your GP or visit a clinic or Brook Advisory Centre and ask them for a test. That way you'll be assured of getting good sympathetic advice whatever the result is. Many girls are scared of visiting their GPs in this situation for fear that they will tell their parents, but new guidelines from the British Medical Association make it quite clear that whether the girl is over or under 16 the consultation should be kept totally confidential, i.e. private. If you are ever in any doubt about this, you should ask, 'Is what we discuss confidential?'

Sometimes you'll see advertisements in local magazines and newspapers for pregnancy testing services run as charities. Often these are associated with anti-abortion organizations who will give you a pregnancy test but will apply a great deal of emotional and moral pressure on you to keep the baby or give it up for adoption. If this is what you want then that's fine, but you may feel more comfortable having less biased advice so that you can make your own decision in your own time.

Step 3: Ask for help.

Carrie's story above showed how dangerous it can be not to get medical advice early on in a pregnancy. But you also need some emotional support. If you find you're pregnant then it's very, very important to tell someone you trust as soon as possible. Your boyfriend may be the first person you turn to, but remember it could be an almighty shock for him and, however much he loves you, he may not be able to offer you the support you need. Telling your mum or another adult might seem like the end of the world and, admittedly, some parents do go over the top and act in the most heartless ways towards their kids in times of crisis. But most families (particularly mothers) do come up trumps.

113

Ellen's Story

I think I knew I was pregnant straight away. My boyfriend and I had been having sex for about six weeks and we usually used a condom, but on this occasion he'd run out and we thought it just wouldn't matter for once. Almost immediately afterwards I started to worry and when my period didn't turn up it was almost a relief to know that my worries were likely to be proved true. I didn't do anything for a couple of weeks, didn't even tell my boyfriend. But eventually when I'd missed my second period I went to a chemist and bought a test kit. I did it at home and sure enough it was positive.

My first thought was how on earth I was going to tell my mum. I knew it would break her heart and also knew she'd go completely crazy. The daughter of one of her friends got pregnant last year, and she went on and on about how terrible it was and how she'd kill me and my sister if it ever happened to us. But I was also scared about what was going to happen, and I knew she'd find out sooner or later and it would be even worse if she thought I hadn't been able to tell her. So, one evening after supper I was helping her stack the dishes when I said, 'Mum, I've got something to tell you.' I think she almost guessed because she sat down and went really pale.

When I told her I thought she was going to hit me, but instead she looked at me for a few moments and then gave me a great big hug and then we both burst into tears. She's been great. She is disappointed, but I don't know how I'd have coped without her. She told my dad and the rest of the family and has kept him off my back, and she took me to the doctor the very next day and is helping me sort out what I'm going to do next.

Ellen, aged 16

Suzanne's Story

Last Sunday I went to see this friend of mine who I used to live near. He's a good bloke and we get on really well and his parents were away on holiday, so one thing led to another and we had sex. The thing is, although we used a condom, I'm terrified I might be pregnant because afterwards we were lying next to each other and it kind of went in again and this time the condom wasn't on.

I felt so awful that when I arrived home I confessed everything to my mum. She's really good about me having sex and stuff; she even buys me condoms! She told me that I'd be all right and that we'd deal with it if it came to that.

Suzanne

Ellen dreaded telling her mum but was surprised to find how supportive she was. Suzanne already knew that her mum would help her no matter what. But not all parents can be guaranteed to respond like this. You know your own parents best and if you really can't face telling them, do talk to a doctor or somebody at a clinic or counselling service. They'll be able to help you and will often act as a go-between, even breaking the news to your parents for you – if that's what you want. Don't be scared they'll rush off and tell people without your permission, because they should always consult you first. Their priority is your emotional and physical health, so they'll do everything they can to make it easier for you.

Step 4: Make your own decisions.

It would be pretty futile and unfair of me to pretend that making any kind of decision when you're pregnant is easy. First of all you often feel fairly grotty and secondly, everybody seems to have their own view on what you should do. Some parents are dead set against abortion, while others take the view that continuing with the pregnancy would ruin your life and they more or less want to wheel you into the operating theatre themselves.

On top of all this you only have a short time to make your mind up about what you're going to do, because if you are going to have an abortion, the earlier you have it, the easier it is. (The majority of abortions take place before the 16th week of pregnancy anyway.) Remember pregnancy is measured from the first day of your last period – not from when you had sex – so by the time you find out you're pregnant you may only have a couple of months in which to act. Abortions are technically legal until the 24th week, but they're only usually carried out at this date if there are severe abnormalities detected in the developing baby.

So everybody's telling you what you ought to do and all you want is to lie down in a cool dark room. How on earth can you reach a decision? Well, there is very good counselling available from organizations like Brook Advisory Centres and the British Pregnancy Advisory Service. Both of them are able to arrange abortions for you, but they're in no way geared up to push you into them against your will. They can help you look at the options for and against, and explain what help would be available to you if you decide to keep the baby. They'll help you separate your own thoughts from everybody else's wishes, so that you get a chance to make up your own mind.

It isn't only parents who try to make your decisions for you: boyfriends can also act in surprising ways. Technically and legally a man does not have a say in whether or not his pregnant partner has a termination, but that doesn't stop blokes having very strong feelings and making their views felt. When you're pregnant and feeling vulnerable this can be overwhelming.

Lorna's Story

My boyfriend and I had been together for eighteen months when I discovered I was pregnant. I'd had a false alarm before and hadn't told him, but this time I knew he had to know. We were a good couple and I thought it was going to last, so I suppose I reckoned that we'd just have the baby and then sort out our lives afterwards. I couldn't have been more wrong. When I told him he immediately started talking about how much an abortion would cost and what he had in the bank. I couldn't believe it. I told him that I wanted to keep the baby and he couldn't believe that either. We talked and talked and eventually he agreed and said he'd stand by me, but from that day things started to chill off.

He was always busy and seemed to forget to phone me until, when I was three months pregnant, he came round one night and started crying and saying that he wanted us to be like we'd been before and he couldn't bear the thought of us having a child. He begged me to have an abortion so that we could start again and maybe have children in the future. I felt so bad about things that I agreed and went to a clinic the next day to see a doctor and ask for an abortion. The final appointment was made for ten days later, and during that time he was really nice to me, taking me out, bringing me flowers etc. I just felt awful.

The day came and he drove me to the clinic, then they showed me to my bed. I just started crying, and when they came round to get me ready for the operation I knew I couldn't do it and I told them I wouldn't go through with it. They were actually really nice about it and took me into a room on my own. Somebody came to talk to me. They didn't try to force me into it or anything, and I called a cab and came home.

When I told my boyfriend he couldn't believe it. He looked as though he was going to shout at me, then he turned round and walked out. I tried to talk to him on the phone after that but he just refused to have anything to do with me and I didn't see him again until the day I had my little girl. My parents were great and my mum was with me during the birth and I suppose she must have rung him up afterwards.

He came into the hospital and stood by the bed, said hello and wasn't the baby lovely and really looked quite pleased with himself. He said he'd see me when I came home, but three months have gone by and I've never heard from him. I was out with the baby in a pushchair the other day and he saw us and crossed over the road to avoid us. I guess that's it – she's not going to have a father, but she does have a mum and grandparents who really love her.

Lorna, aged 17

Carol was 21 when she got pregnant and had a totally different experience. She had met her partner Paul through his sister when she'd moved down to London to work, and although he was a lot older he seemed an ideal partner. They went out for a few months and then Carol left the job she was in and joined Paul's company and began living with him.

Carol's Story

Things were fine for a while and then I discovered I was expecting. It really hurt me that Paul would not give me time to adjust to the situation. I felt that I was trapping myself and him. At the time my parents didn't know I was with him and I needed time to tell them.

Paul was a lot older than me and came from quite a well-to-do family, and he refused to allow 'his child' to be born illegitimate and so arranged our wedding. We married and I felt trapped and resented the baby I was carrying. On Christmas Eve that year I walked out and came back up North. Mum and Dad didn't know and I was able to hide my pregnancy. In the February I gave birth to a son who I gave to Paul.

Later that year we put in for a divorce and the split was legalized. Paul got his son and even after all the heartbreak and the hate, bitterness, self-loathing and other people's sneers, I still know that Paul and I are better off away from each other. People tend to think that I was cold and hard for giving up my son, but they didn't know or feel the way I did.

Carol

Step 5: Ask for more help.

Whatever decision you make, things are still going to be hard, so do ask for more help and get as much support as you possibly can. Having an abortion may seem like an easy option to some people, but it is traumatic and many people feel depressed for a long time afterwards. If your family or boyfriend were in favour of the abortion then they may want to sweep everything under the carpet afterwards and pretend that nothing happened. They may expect you to go along with this and be jolly and happy when all you want to do is cry.

It's hard for them to understand but it's very important that you have a chance to talk about your feelings with someone who does sympathize. Most abortion clinics offer post-abortion counselling services after the operation, but you can also go to a Brook Advisory Centre or contact the Post Abortion Counselling Service (see 'Resources'), enclosing an s.a.e.

Many girls find it hard to resume their sexual relationships after an abortion because they associate sex with the emotional pain they've gone through. Often this dies away with tender loving care, but if it persists then it's a good idea to talk to a counsellor about your relationship and the feelings that you may be trying to hide. If you need more time from your partner then for heaven's sake say so. Men aren't the best mind-readers in the world and they don't know what you're going through unless you tell them.

Having a baby is hardly an easy option either. Whether you keep it or give it up for adoption you are going to feel very different and under a great deal of stress. Again, don't be scared to ask for help. If you keep your baby the health visitor from your GP practice will come and see you a couple of weeks after the birth, and you can always contact her if you're feeling down or lonely or frightened. She should be able to put you in touch with some other new mums' groups and sort out some practical and financial help too if necessary. You can look in the 'Resources' section at the back of the book for some other organizations that help new mums.

I had just turned 16 when I had my baby and I had already decided to leave school. At first I thought I'd just stay at home, but my mum was great and said that she'd look after the baby while I went on a YTS course. My local careers officer gave me advice about courses and it made the world of difference to me. It wasn't easy because I still had to get up in the night and look after Jonathan whenever he woke up, so I was tired all the time, but I know I could never have made it without the support of my mum.
Miranda

There was never any question of me having an abortion – I just don't agree with them. But I knew I wouldn't be able to stay at home and have the baby. I've never got on with my stepdad and I was already having to share a room with one of my younger brothers.

I assumed at first I'd get council housing but even though single mums do get preferential treatment (or so they say) I was told it would be ages before I could expect my own place. In fact to get anything I had to be actually homeless which meant being out on the streets. I spent one or two nights sleeping on park benches and sheltering under bushes when I was about seven months pregnant. It was very scary but I was desperate and I didn't know what else to do.

Then Social Services put me in a bed and breakfast place and I'm still there now with my little girl. There's no way anybody could call it home. We're in a small, damp room and we share a loo and a kitchen with lots of other families, some with as many as four or five children. I try to get out as much as I can with her, but when the weather is bad we're stuck in. I can't even afford the bus fare to visit my mum more than once a week.

Rowena

Whatever you might read in the papers there's no automatic safety net to look after young single mothers and their children. You're certainly very unlikely to be offered the keys to a council flat just like that, and many girls in this situation find themselves living in pretty awful conditions. They may be desperate to get away from home, but the reality of life on their own still comes as a shock. Finding your way around the benefits system can be like negotiating a maze, so it's vital that you get all the help you can and make sure you use every bit of aid available to you. For more information, see the section on pregnancy in chapter nine, Rights and Wrongs, and also the 'Resources' section at the back of the book.

If you think you might be pregnant

THE EMERGENCY CONTRACEPTIVE PILL IS AVAILABLE UP UNTIL **3 DAYS (72 HOURS)** AFTER UNPROTECTED SEX.

SOMETIMES AN IUD CAN BE FITTED UP UNTIL 5 DAYS AFTER — AVAILABLE FROM G.P.s, FAMILY PLANNING CLINICS, BROOK ADVISORY CENTRES ETC.

PREGNANCY TESTS CAN BE DONE FROM THE FIRST DAY YOUR NEXT PERIOD IS DUE — AVAILABLE FROM G.P.s AND CLINICS, OR BUY A D.I.Y. TEST KIT FROM A CHEMIST.

IF YOU ARE PREGNANT IT'S VITAL YOU TELL SOMEONE YOU TRUST AS SOON AS POSSIBLE. REMEMBER CLINICS AND DOCTORS CAN HELP YOU WORK OUT HOW TO TELL YOUR PARENTS AND/OR BOYFRIEND.

IT MAY BE HARD IF EVERYONE IS TELLING YOU WHAT THEY THINK YOU OUGHT TO DO, BUT YOU ARE THE ONE WHO HAS TO DECIDE WHAT'S RIGHT FOR YOU.

WHATEVER YOU DECIDE, THINGS ARE STILL GOING TO BE DIFFICULT SO MAKE SURE YOU GET AS MUCH HELP AS YOU CAN. LOOK IN THE RESOURCES CHAPTER FOR SUGGESTIONS.

1.
It may not be too late for emergency contraception.

2.
Find out if you really are pregnant.

3.
Ask for help.

4.
Make your own decisions.

5.
Ask for more help.

Chapter Six

Getting Stuck
COPING WITH EMOTIONAL BLACKMAIL
AND THE FEAR OF LONELINESS

When I was writing this book I dreaded getting to this chapter because I knew the cynical old hag at the heart of me would be revealed. This chapter is about why we stay in grotty, depressing and damaging relationships and, more particularly, how people find the courage to leave them.

So here's the cynical bit. Skip over the next paragraph if you're madly in love and know that nothing bad will ever happen to you. But, in my experience, what I'm about to say is the truth.

Life is not a fairy tale. We may grow up relishing the thought of Cinderella and the Prince living happily ever after in their castle on the hill, but unless we can accept a more realistic view of our own relationships we are likely to end up being very unhappy indeed.

Love is *wonderful*. It pulls people together and it makes the whole world shine. But time doesn't stand still there. People grow and people change and this puts strains on even the best relationship. When things are basically good the relationship will change and develop too and become stronger because of it. Nevertheless all relationships have bad moments and even the happiest couple will have both thought of jumping ship at some point over the years. The factor that probably keeps them together is the knowledge that the good outweighs the bad. It's worth putting up with a bit of pain and distress to nurture something that has given you so much pleasure in the past. And should do in the future. But that doesn't make it easy. The situation I want to discuss here is the relationship where, for at least one partner, the bad heavily outweighs the good. Of course, in most cases this simply signals the unavoidable and the eventual break-up of the relationship – but breaking up is never easy.

Tamsin's Story

Eight years ago I was nearly pushed into a relationship. When I was at school I met this guy. We were together for over five years until I was 20. He was nice enough, but he didn't have anything going for him, as I found out later. He became very dependent on me as he didn't have a lot of friends and just a small family, and he begrudged me a lot of things (friends, nights out, exams for my career as a secretary), and he sulked a lot, which made me feel guilty. We got engaged when I was 18 but didn't get round to saving for a wedding or a home of our own as we were always making plans but never carrying them out.

As the relationship went on I began to feel I was getting into a 'going nowhere' routine and I felt dragged down. Was this how it was going to be for our future? I kept thinking of his begrudgingly immature attitude, with me giving in and plodding along, never doing anything or going anywhere. In other words a bored, lonely, intimidated housewife. I was determined this wasn't going to happen to me and I wanted more out of life. I knew that the relationship had gone stale, but it was so hard trying to finish with him as he clung on and made me feel guilty – and I suppose I did love him still.

The problem was my family adored him. He stayed for weeks at a time and became like a brother and son to them. He could do no wrong. As my feelings had changed I began to withdraw from him. I became irritable, my love for him was fizzling out and I knew I had to do something soon.

We had a huge row one day because I'd asked to have a girls' night out. Believe me, I hated having to ask but I felt I needed to get out with friends. I'd let them down too many times because of him, but I'm a great believer in still having time for friends even when in a relationship, so this time I decided to go. He hit the roof and said it was him or my friends. I was disgusted that he could make me choose like this and it showed me how immature he really was. I chose my friends and finished with him that day. I'd had enough.

Do you think Tamsin was silly to throw away a relationship for the sake of a night out? What would you have done?

Tamsin knew that things weren't right and she spent many long months brooding about how she could escape, while all the time her family and boyfriend built up this picture of the perfect rosy relationship around her. It was one incident that made her crack and tell him that things were over. But it wasn't that easy for her and I'll tell you a bit more of Tamsin's story later on.

So why do people stay month after month, year after year, in a relationship that causes them such pain? I think there are two main reasons:

1. Emotional blackmail
2. Fear of loneliness

These problems afflict both sexes as you can see from these letters.

EMOTIONAL BLACKMAIL

I'm 15 and have been going out with my girlfriend for just over two years. She's the only girl I've ever been out with. I suppose I do love her but lately things haven't been very good between us. Whenever we talk we end up fighting and it usually ends up my fault. I've suggested we break up for a while but she started crying and making me feel guilty for even suggesting such a thing. She's said she couldn't live without me, even though it would only be a trial separation.

128

I realize that I would miss her badly if we ever did break up, but the relationship has lost all its sparkle. Also all my friends tell me I'm mad to be going steady at such a young age and that I'd be better off 'playing the field' like the rest of them. I'm beginning to think they might be right, but I'm so confused.

Phil

I'm 16 and I have a big problem. I'm going out with a 17-year-old boy but I don't love him as much as I used to. He gets angry with me and swears and frightens me. He says he does this because he loves me. Sometimes he's nice and he's always like that to other people when they're around, so they all think he's wonderful and stick up for him.

About three years ago I went out very briefly with a boy who lives just round the corner. Lately I've been hanging round with him and I've got off with him behind my boyfriend's back. I really like this boy and he seems to like me and treats me with respect, unlike my boyfriend. However, he says that I should give my boyfriend another chance, but I just can't stand it.

I've tried telling my boyfriend that I want to end it, but I can't as he falls to pieces and cries and gets down on his knees and makes me feel so heartless. He says he loves me. I've given him loads of other chances but he always goes back to his normal self. I don't know what I can do as I can't talk to my mum because she thinks my boyfriend is lovely and says the other boy is just trying to break us up.

Michelle

I've always felt that I've been pushed into relationships. I got married when I was 16 and pregnant and only managed to get a divorce after six very violent years. After a few years on my own I met someone else but he too turned out to be violent and it was very hard to get away from him.

My third and final try at settling down has just ended in divorce. He left me alone for a couple of years, but then as soon as my divorce came through, the trouble began. My ex-husband waits for me going to work and jumps out of bushes. He also says that he's going to kill himself if I don't have him back. He was constantly phoning me so I've had to change my number which I

can now give to nobody. The only way he will leave me alone is if I agree to meet him a couple of times a week, and he won't accept that I don't want any kind of relationship with him. When I try to tell him that what he's doing to me is blackmail, he makes my life hell unless I agree to do what he says. I won't give in to his demands but I have very little help legally because it's not as though he was beating me up or anything.

Sandra

All of these people are suffering from the threats and demands of their partners. If we could talk to those partners they'd probably tell us that they only do it because they love them. But love, unfortunately, doesn't have the power to make everything right. For a relationship to be successful, the people in it have to stay in it of their own free will, not because they're scared of what will happen if they leave. It can be very hard to accept this if you are desperately in love and feel that the object of your affections would really, should really, love you too if only you could show them the way. You feel that your love is enough for the two of you and can't understand why they don't just give in and accept it.

It feels rather different on the receiving end. A part of you may indeed love the other person, but all these emotional demands and threats get in the way. In terms of power they control everything, although that probably isn't how they see it.

John said that he and his girlfriend always ended up fighting and he thought it was his fault. That made him feel guilty so he tended to stay and put up with things that bit longer. In fact the rows were probably his way of trying to claw back some of the power in the relationship and make himself feel a bit more comfortable. Subconsciously he was probably also hoping that she would get fed up with the arguing and break off with him.

That's quite a common situation. One partner wants to leave but doesn't want to be seen as causing the split, so they try to provoke the other partner into leaving instead. It may seem like an act of kindness but it often makes things drag on a lot longer than they would if you were simply honest from the start. Michelle is stuck with a boy who treats her very badly. She's got her eye on another boy and has even started going out with him, but she's still with her boyfriend because he makes her feel so guilty every time she raises the subject of splitting up. Of course, sooner or later he'll find out that she's seeing someone else and he'll be even more hurt. There will be further tears and reconciliations but there's no way they'll ever get back together as a happy couple. In other words it would be much kinder to put a stop to things now.

Sandra shows what can happen when you don't learn to say what you mean. She has now had three repetitive relationships where violence or coercion have played a major role. Here she is, divorced from her third partner, yet still living her life in fear because of his emotional blackmail. She ends up agreeing to meet him a couple of times a week just for the sake of some peace. As long as she does this she encourages his belief that, deep down, she really wants to be with him. So he goes on pushing and forcing her.

She could take legal action against him – not pleasant I know – but she chooses not to because she doesn't want to 'hurt' him. It's as though the two of them are locked in a game, pressing each other's buttons. The more he chases her, the worse she feels and the more likely she is to give in to him. As long as she gives in every now and then, he feels justified in continuing to lay on the pressure. And so it goes on.

HOW TO COPE WITH EMOTIONAL BLACKMAIL

Step 1: Accept that you are responsible for your own feelings.

Being on the receiving end of emotional blackmail isn't pleasant and you probably don't like what the other person is doing to you. But you can't put all the blame on them. You have a choice to go or stay. And by remaining in the relationship you allow it to go on happening. Concentrate less on how your partner is acting and more on how you feel about the way things are going. If your discomfort and unhappiness outweigh the pleasure you get from the relationship then it's time to take action.

Step 2: Understand that the other person must also take responsibility for their own feelings.

Emotional blackmail is scary because it makes you fear what the other person will do. Their overload of pain and loneliness washes over you, making you feel responsible for whatever might happen. But you can't control someone else's life. And you shouldn't make your own life miserable simply for fear that they can't cope without you. They have a problem, and unless they get to grips with it they will always be unhappy. Their situation with you is likely to repeat itself with other partners. You may be able to help them see this, but you won't make things any better by hanging on in there when you know there is no future in it.

Step 3: If you're going to go, then go.

Make it clear, preferably face to face, that you can't continue and that you want to call a halt to the relationship. This is probably your worst nightmare because every emotional stop will be pulled and you'll feel lower than ever. But remember, you're doing this to save both of you increasing future pain, so stick to your guns, say what you mean and walk away.

Step 4: Stand by your decision.

There will be many pleas, phone calls, letters and 'accidental-on-purpose' meetings where you may feel tempted to get back together for a bit just to ease the pain. *Don't do it*. Any encouragement is irresponsible as it will only allow your partner to assume there is hope of a reconciliation.

How do you know they won't do something silly?

Remember what I said about each of you being responsible for your own feelings? Well, by walking out you are allowing your ex-partner to get to grips with his or her own feelings. The fact is, whatever they threatened it's very unlikely they will harm themselves. But if you think there is a possibility, then it's fair to warn someone close to them of your decision to split up before you do it. Be careful of this, because it's never pleasant for someone to find out that they were the last to know that their relationship was over, but talking to their mum, big sister or best friend can help ensure there's a loving shoulder and a watchful eye ready and waiting when you walk out that door.

If you're really worried, it might be a good idea to find the address and phone number of your local counselling service (see the 'Resources' chapter) and offer it to your ex or their mum or whoever, suggesting that a few support sessions might be in order. You could use this too – ending a relationship is never easy and what you're doing takes a lot of courage and emotional energy. Don't be scared to ask for some advice and support.

Coping with emotional blackmail

YOU CAN ALWAYS CHOOSE WHETHER TO STAY IN A RELATIONSHIP OR NOT. AND IF IT'S CAUSING YOU A LOT OF PAIN — MAYBE YOU HAVEN'T MADE THE RIGHT CHOICE!

YOU WON'T MAKE THINGS ANY BETTER BY HANGING ON JUST BECAUSE YOU'RE SCARED OF HOW THEY'LL COPE WITHOUT YOU.

THE LONGER YOU PUT IT OFF THE WORSE IT WILL BE — FOR BOTH OF YOU.

IT WASN'T EASY TO REACH THIS DECISION BUT IT WILL ALL HAVE BEEN FOR NOTHING IF YOU GIVE IN AGAIN TO EMOTIONAL BLACKMAIL.

1.
Accept that you are responsible for your own feelings.

2.
Understand that the other person must also take responsibility for their own feelings.

3.
If you're going to go, then go.

4.
Stand by your decision.

FEAR OF LONELINESS

The fear of being on your own can lead you into some pretty desperate action. When the thought of losing your partner fills you with panic and terror you may be prepared to try just about anything to keep the relationship going.

Nicola's Story

I'm now 16 years old, mature for that age as I've been through a lot. I'm desperately unhappy with my life and I feel like topping myself when things get too much. This is something I would never do, but I just crave for a way out of everything. I feel so let down and would have given up long ago if I hadn't met my boyfriend. He helped me through everything, but finds it hard to understand the way I feel about some things. I met him on holiday but we don't live that far away. We didn't actually get off together at first as he's too nice for that.

I didn't want to rush things. I did though, and within three months I'd dropped all my friends from school and outside school and saw my boyfriend every night and day. He gave up his friends, although we do see a couple of his mates for one evening a week. I've tied him and myself down and I can't get out.

I have no life other than with him. I don't go out and if I'm not with him I sit at home. I'm getting worse as I really need to move out from home as my mum and I row all the time and she keeps threatening to kick me out. I'm putting my boyfriend under pressure to get a flat with me but he won't as he's got a nice house and a great family, but I still go on about marriage and kids even though I know that we'd argue too much. We do feel right for each other, but I'm so scared of what might happen if we ever fall out that I won't ever sit back and think if we're really suited or is this going anywhere. We've been together over a year and things are getting worse. I don't even see people from my old school.

I ask him personal questions all the time about his

ex-girlfriend and his past and I blame him for everything he did before he met me, which I know is wrong.

I don't trust him at all, although I know he's trustworthy to a T. I won't let him go out with anyone although he's only ever asked to once in the last year, and I'm scared that he'll meet someone else, someone thin and pretty with a nice house and a rich family.

I've become totally dependent on him and would just rot away without him, and I'm always thinking of ways to 'catch' him and make sure that he never leaves. I know this isn't right and I desperately need a life of my own, but I just don't know what to do. I have nothing but him.

Nicola

Rob's Story

I met my girlfriend in my second year at college. I'd always been a loner and didn't fit easily into any 'group'. She was a new first year student and just seemed so pretty and gentle, totally unlike all the others. I remember how she smiled when I first spoke to her and I couldn't believe my luck when she agreed to go out with me.

We were together for nearly six months and every second was wonderful. We never rowed and I always did everything that she wanted and spent all my time trying to make sure things were great for her. So I couldn't believe it when one day she said she had something to tell me. She wanted us to break up, even though she assured me there was nobody else. She said it was interfering with her studying and that she wanted some time on her own. I could understand this and I offered over and over again to give her more freedom just as long as I could see her at least once a week. The thought of her being with anyone else killed me but I knew I could not have her all to myself.

We broke up for about two weeks, but then I couldn't bear it and during the holidays I hitched down to her home town and told her I couldn't stand it any more. We got back together, but it only lasted another couple of weeks before she said she didn't want to see me at all. It broke my heart because I knew that if only she could understand how much I loved her, I could make her so happy. I found myself walking past her digs and writing to her every day. Every so often she would agree to meet me but it always ended up with the same argument. I just couldn't understand how she could turn her back on something as good as what we had.

Rob, aged 20

Gillian's Story

For the past eight months I've been seeing a married man who is no longer with his wife (because of our relationship) and although all along I've known it isn't what I want, I find it hard to keep away. This isn't because I'm madly in love with him (although I am fond of him), it just seems at the moment that I'd rather be in this relationship than totally on my own. I'm disgusted with myself for breaking up his marriage, which isn't what I wanted. In fact I wish he was still with her and have basically always felt that way. Only last week I broke it off, but within two days was seeing him again. It feels to me that it's mainly through habit but also because he's the only love and stability in my life at the moment. To me the whole relationship isn't what I want and has had quite a few bad times. We have very different views on life, religion, etc. and he's very racist and cannot handle the fact that I've mainly been out with black guys.

I suppose I got into the relationship because I was vulnerable and had been suffering from depression, but he's always been very supportive and loving, helping me first into my own flat and then to redecorate it amongst other things. Also I know I can be a pain and am a fiery person with a hot temper. There have been times when I've been so angry about our relationship and his hurtful remarks that I've been determined to leave, yet I'm still with him and am beginning to wonder what it would take to finish it. At the moment anger, hurt, resentment and the knowledge that we're just not suited doesn't seem enough, and my life is completely out of control.

Gillian

Have you ever felt terrified that your boyfriend or girlfriend would leave you? Which was the most scary – the thought of losing them or of being on your own?

All of these people are hanging on to a relationship that, realistically, is past its sell-by date. Nicola and Gillian have a fair degree of insight and understand that they are opting for a less than satisfactory love affair because the alternative of being on their own is too hard to contemplate. Interestingly it's Rob (whose girlfriend has already said she doesn't want to continue) who has the least insight but still thinks that the power of his love will keep them together. I'll tell you a bit more about Rob later.

Learning to let go

So if you're in this position is there anything that can be done to salvage and even improve the relationship? Well there's no guaranteed, sure-fire way of sticking things back together because by the time things get to this point most relationships are past saving. But the following steps can give you a fighting chance.

Step 1: Understand that your possessive behaviour and emotional demands will destroy things later if not much sooner.

If you don't believe me, read the earlier letters from the people who thought they were being emotionally blackmailed. If you carry on like this you will drive your love away. End of story.

Step 2: Take a deep breath and let go a little.

You can't change your behaviour overnight, but for one afternoon or one evening, or even a whole Saturday or Sunday, you should turn your back on your beloved and do something for *you*. OK, I know all you want to do is lie on their doorstep and wail, but that's off-limits for the moment. Go and see an old friend, visit your gran, offer to clean the family car or, even better, go swimming or take a long walk. Do something that makes you feel good and has nothing to do with them at all. Don't ruin it by starting a

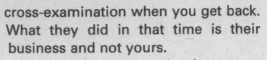

cross-examination when you get back. What they did in that time is their business and not yours.

Now make it a regular feature: at least once a week take time out for yourself. I can't guarantee this will save things, but if your relationship hasn't already gone down the pan there's a chance this will slow its decline slightly by taking the pressure off your partner and showing them that there is a glimmer of hope that you might change into a more rational human being.

Step 3: Talk to someone.

No, I don't mean your boyfriend or girlfriend, but I do mean a helpful and sympathetic adult. Maybe your mum or a teacher or your best friend's mum or dad, but find someone who will listen to you and let you pour out your pain and anger. Young people's counselling services can be invaluable in this position and I strongly suggest you find out the closest one and get in touch with them. Explain you want to talk to a counsellor about a relationship problem. Look in the 'Resources' section at the back of this book for details of finding more information on this.

Learning to let go

THE PERSON YOU LOVE CAN BE SCARED BY THE INTENSITY OF YOUR EMOTIONS. IF YOU GO ON LIKE THIS YOU WILL DRIVE THEM AWAY.

1.
Understand that your possessive behaviour will destroy your relationship.

GIVE YOURSELF A BREAK (EVEN IF ONLY A COUPLE OF HOURS) FROM ALL THE HEARTACHE AND WORRY. DO SOMETHING NICE FOR YOU.

2.
Take a deep breath and let go a little.

YOU MAY BE FEELING CONFUSED, ANGRY, SCARED OR A WHOLE MIXTURE OF EMOTIONS BUT YOU'LL FEEL A LOT BETTER IF YOU CAN SHARE IT WITH SOMEONE OUTSIDE THE RELATIONSHIP.

3.
Talk to someone.

CAN YOU LIVE HAPPILY EVER AFTER?

I can't make any promises, but with the right attitude and proper help you can survive this sort of crisis. Take Rob for example. He was desperately in love, but his girlfriend had had enough, and yet he still hounded her. This is what happened.

One day there was a message for me at college saying I was to see my personal supervisor urgently. When I got there he told me that my girlfriend had made a complaint to the college authorities and there was a possibility she was going to take legal action to keep me away from her. I couldn't believe it. I thought my world had fallen apart. Luckily he was really sympathetic and instead of screaming at me, he sat and listened to me for a long time and suggested that I see one of the college counsellors. He rang and made an appointment and took me along there almost immediately.

It hasn't been easy, but I spent a lot of time talking and thinking about what went on and I see now that I was fooling myself. At first I really thought I was going crazy and I didn't see any way out of it. But with the counsellor's help I began to understand that although my view of the relationship might never have been realistic, it was understandable taken in terms of my own past. My mum and dad had always rowed a lot and my mum kept threatening to walk out. All through my childhood I was terrified of the next big argument, and I can see now it was that sense of insecurity that led me to hang on to my girlfriend the way I did.

Life is a lot easier now. Of course I still think of her, but I do other things and although I haven't yet had another serious relationship, I do have some girls who are good friends, which I think is a move in the right direction.

To anyone else in that situation, I'd just like to say that I know how hard it is to let go, but you have to understand that you're fooling yourself and killing the love between you by trying to hold on to someone against their will. There simply is no way you can force someone to love you.

So Rob made it and although he knows that life isn't easy, he is hopeful for the future.

At the beginning of this chapter I told you about Tamsin, who found herself in a relationship she resented with a boyfriend who was so possessive she wasn't ever supposed to see her own friends. The last straw came when she tried to get out for one day and he gave her an ultimatum, saying it was him or them. She chose her friends and finished with him. But it wasn't that easy.

I finished with him that day as I'd had enough. However, my mum and brothers had heard the commotion and they turned on me, saying that I was losing a good lad and that I'd been so moody lately I couldn't possibly know what I was doing. In the end, to keep the peace, I took him back. The grin on his face when he knew he'd won and that I wouldn't get to have my night out and my family had turned against me, summed it all up for me. I would bide my time, but it was over! I didn't ever want to go through this again. What right did he have to do this to me? I could see my worst fears being realized and I knew I had to do something fast, because if I didn't change my future, nobody else would.

He had to go out of town one day so I took my chance to have a girls' night out. I desperately needed a fun night with friends. While I was out I had such a good time that I knew there was more of a life for me out there and I just had to find it. A few days later while my brothers were out of the house, I took my mum aside and told her I was going to finish with him. I explained it all to her and she said she hadn't realized I was so unhappy and that she only stepped in the last time because she really did think that I was just 'going through a stage'.

I finished with him that night. No fuss or bother – just took a deep breath and ended it. The relief was tremendous. He cried and begged me to go back to him for weeks afterwards but I wouldn't give an inch. I knew I had to stick to my guns and I did. The huge black cloud that had been over my head was gone for good and I felt wonderful.

I went on holiday with friends, had many nights out and did a lot of things I hadn't done in ages. It was such fun. I felt as if I was living again. Six months later I met a wonderful guy and we had so much in common that we fell in love easily. We've been married for five years now and are very happy indeed. We both have wonderful jobs, we have time for our friends with no jealous hang-ups, and are now hoping to complete our happiness by trying for a family.

Chapter Seven

Let's Make This Our Secret
COPING WITH ABUSIVE RELATIONSHIPS

What's the difference between keeping something private and making it a secret?

Secret and private are two words which may mean much the same thing but, to me, they have quite a different flavour. Many people quite naturally want to keep their relationships private. Love, not to mention sex, is intensely personal, and the last thing you want is everyone from the milkman to Aunt Mabel sticking their nose in asking how it's going. But I think the word *secret* has a more ominous flavour. A secret relationship is one which the rest of the world might not approve of. The sort of relationship which other people would want to stop.

The secret relationships I'm talking about here are those where power is abused. We've already looked at emotional blackmail and how boyfriends and girlfriends can bring pressure to bear to make partners sleep with them or stay with them or even get engaged or married. Those are difficult situations but they essentially happen between two people who have more or less equal power. Other relationships

take place between couples who are on very different rungs of the power ladder. One is usually older and may be in a position of authority, e.g. parent, relation, teacher, boss. They may use that authority to attract and control a younger person and then abuse it by starting the sort of behaviour which will eventually damage their victim.

In the last few years there has been increasing publicity about sexual abuse and incest. This is a major problem and I have many letters in my postbag every week from young people who are being repeatedly abused. But there are other kinds of damaging, secret relationships. These range from the teacher who stands too close and makes personal comments, the uncle who insists on kissing you goodbye 'properly', and the boss who keeps you working late and gives you a lift home only to stop in a deserted lay-by.

Many of the people who write to me complaining of these sorts of situations wonder whether they really have a right to feel uncomfortable about what's happening. They know something feels wrong but they're scared that if they make a fuss, other people will laugh at them or not believe them, or they'll get into trouble. And this, of course is exactly what the abuser counts on. By taking things slowly and gradually, the abuser leads, persuades or blackmails the victim (and they are victims) into going further and further until they're terrified to tell anyone for fear of admitting what they themselves have done.

If someone you liked and respected started making personal remarks and touching you, how would you feel? Can you imagine telling them to stop? Would you be able to confide in anyone else?

PERSONAL SPACE

We are all surrounded by an invisible area of personal space. If someone steps into it uninvited you feel uncomfortable.

Lovers walk along the road with their arms around each other or sit close together on sofas. Friends huddle together over a desk to look at something. This isn't uncomfortable because they're people you know and trust and you're happy to have them close to you. But think of a crowded train. People are crammed into seats and standing in corridors and aisles. You're jammed between two strangers with their thighs touching yours. This does *not* feel comfortable. They are invading your personal space and you're doing the same to them. Because there's no choice, people look straight ahead and avoid eye contact, or bury their noses in a book. This helps lessen the discomfort.

Children don't have this notion of personal space; it's something that comes on us as we grow up. Some people reject it or, perhaps because they have mental or social problems, don't acknowledge it. You may have met someone like this, who on being introduced to you stands very close and tends to look straight into your eyes a lot. This can be a sign of attraction but if the feeling isn't mutual it's very confusing. It also feels threatening.

THE RIGHT TO RESPECT

In any relationship you have a right to respect. That means you don't expect another person to invade your space unless you feel comfortable with them, nor should they make personal or embarrassing comments unless you are able to do the same to them. In other words it's OK for friends to make fun of each other because you're on an equal level and you can get your own back. But a teacher who starts making intimate and embarrassing comments about a pupil is abusing their position. The pupil feels uncomfortable, but can't answer back without being accused of rudeness.

A while ago I received this letter from a group of twelve girls in one form at school.

Our problem is our French teacher. He's in his fifties and repulsive. He often leers over the girls in our class. He stands very close to us, putting his hands on our shoulders or even stroking our backs. He smells, but what's worse is he makes horrible and sometimes suggestive comments. We can't stand him and he makes us feel sick. What can we do?

This man may not be aware that he has a personal hygiene problem, but I'm sure he's getting some kind of kick out of the power he has over these girls. Maybe he likes seeing them embarrassed or perhaps he gets a sexual thrill from saying suggestive things them while he strokes their backs. Either way, he's way out of line and definitely abusing his position.

But it's very hard to do anything about a teacher, isn't it?

Well, yes and no. Certainly saying anything to him would probably be taken as cheek or rudeness and you may just end up being punished or victimized. But in a position like this I would advise the girls to get together and talk to the Head Teacher. They should make a list of the names of all the girls who want to complain, and then a couple of them should make an appointment to talk to the Head about a problem. Once in the Head's office they should avoid moaning (and they certainly shouldn't giggle), but should make a flat statement of complaint saying how uncomfortable his actions make them feel. Taking a logical and calm approach will always encourage an adult to take you seriously. The Head Teacher will ask for examples of the suggestive comments made and they should have these already written down, along with the dates when they were made.

In this situation, the Head should take them seriously and some sort of action will follow. This could be the Head having a quiet word with the teacher concerned, or something more drastic. If things don't get better then the pupils or their parents can take the matter further to the Director of Education in their local education authority. A complaint which reaches this level has to be investigated, but it's always better to try and get things sorted out at a school level, if possible.

Kim is 12 and at boarding school. She suffered the same kind of problem with one of her teachers and luckily, with help from her friends, was able to do something about it.

When I first came to school my maths teacher seemed to be just a very friendly teacher. He started to rub my shoulders and back every time he saw me (like he did to every girl) and I didn't really care at first. But then it happened constantly and he would start rubbing my chest (but not anywhere private) so I began to feel very uncomfortable. I told a couple of my friends and they watched out for me but it still got worse, to the extent that I was terrified to go to his classes and was having nightmares about him. Eventually my friends told me to tell somebody that I trusted so I managed to pluck up courage to talk to another teacher. I was really scared but she was great. She told the Headmaster and the Deputy Head, and the teacher was told to stop doing those sorts of things to girls.

I feel much better and I'd just like to say to anyone else who has this sort of problem that they should tell someone. I know it's hard but I promise it feels better afterwards.

It has to be admitted that not everyone gets such an easy result as Kim. Sometimes teachers (or other adults) don't want to listen. Or, if they feel they are being accused of something, their behaviour may get even worse. But that doesn't mean you should stay silent. Find someone else to tell and keep on doing it, explaining that no one seems to be willing to help, until someone does take you – and your problem – seriously.

BUT I REALLY LIKE HIM

Some victims don't complain about their abuse. On the contrary, they welcome the advances being made and are flattered by the obvious attraction of an older person.

At a family party recently my uncle was kissing and cuddling me. He did this in front of the family. He also wanted to dance with me but I refused. I didn't used to like him and my dad hates him, but at the party I really felt something for him and I think he felt something for me.

He's married and has two children and is 38 years old. I keep thinking about him and can't wait to see him again. When we were cuddling, his wife, my aunt, told him that I was too young for him and that he should leave me alone. I may be exaggerating about him feeling something for me, but I don't think so. I would sleep with him if he asked me – that's how serious I feel about him.

Anne, aged 14

From the sound of things, Anne's uncle has a reputation for leading on young girls. The trouble is, because Anne enjoys it and is excited by his attentions, he could just lead her on too far. It makes a man, particularly a middle-aged man, feel immensely powerful to see a beautiful young and innocent girl go weak at the knees over him. It's very, very tempting for him to take things further and break the unspoken boundaries of their relationship – and in this case Anne would be only too happy to go along with him. He is using his age and his position in the family to lure her into an intimate and possibly sexual relationship. The fact that he does it so openly in front of other members of the family makes her feel that everything must be all right. But it's obvious from her letter that her aunt at least is feeling uneasy about this. And I can't help wondering why her dad can't stand him.

But Anne is in a difficult position, because even if she didn't welcome the kissing and cuddling, most children are brought up to accept this kind of affection from their relations. We've all heard it: 'Kiss your auntie goodbye, give your uncle a big hug.' But I don't believe that children should be forced to kiss and hug adults just for the sake of politeness. It passes the message to the child that it's OK for grown-ups to invade their personal space and touch them, even if it's against their wishes. (See page 221 for a legal definition of child abuse.)

I worry about Anne and people like her a lot. I don't know what will happen to her, but I suspect that unless somebody in her family intervenes, she is going to end up in a sexual relationship if not with her uncle then another older man who may take advantage of her. At the time it may be what she thinks she wants, but the chances are she will be badly hurt.

WHAT IF THE ABUSER IS THE BOSS?

A classic case of a relationship where one person has all the power is the boss and employee. Sexual harassment has become a buzz-word over recent years and it is now illegal, but that doesn't seem to stop it happening. Like many other teenagers Leanne desperately wanted a Saturday job and was prepared to put up with quite a bit of inconvenience in order to keep it.

I'm 16 and I've been here for ten months now. My problem is that my boss is always grabbing my breasts and bottom. He does this to the other girls but only in fun. However, on two occasions he has asked me to go in early to help him. He tells me he loves me. He makes me feel dirty. He is about 35 and married with children. A couple of months ago he drove me home and stopped in an alleyway. He wouldn't stop touching me even when I told him to stop.

The other day at work he asked me to help him put some things in the store room. He shut the door and wouldn't let me go. He was so strong, I told him to get off and I didn't like it, but he kept grabbing and trying to kiss me. I can't tell my mum as they are friends. Is this sexual harassment and what should I do? I threatened to leave before and I told him I would tell about what he's been doing, but he says I've no proof and it's just my imagination. I can't leave.

Leanne

Leanne's boss is definitely in the wrong, but if it's a small company, like a shop, and there's no one else in authority, then her only solution may be to leave. That probably feels like running away, and it does leave her boss in his position of power with the opportunity to abuse endless further Saturday girls – but it's also probably the best route for self-preservation.

I think Leanne certainly should tell her mum, particularly as they are friends. And I think she should also be aware that if he tried to keep her trapped in a car or store room while touching her and kissing her, she could accuse him of sexual assault. He's probably the last person to see himself as a dirty old man and is most likely convinced that Leanne secretly fancies him. A visit from the police might be just what is needed to wake him up to reality. But the end result is still the same – Leanne will almost certainly have to leave.

Another way of coping with things is to draw attention to them immediately. Some adults, particularly men, genuinely don't realize that their behaviour is unpleasant or threatening. It's not easy to handle this in public, but if you work with someone who's a regular bottom-fondler you could try shouting out, 'Oh look, he's grabbing me again' every time he goes for a grope. Like a small child shouting 'NO' when a stranger approaches them, this draws everyone's attention to the problem and makes the groper look pretty foolish. Often the embarrassment is enough to stop the behaviour.

But most important of all, if you are in a situation where your boss is trying to take advantage of you, then you must tell someone what's going on. And you must do it as soon as the problem starts. That way if it does get into a confrontation between you and your boss, you have someone to back you up. If there is another, older female employee then it's likely that she's seen his little tricks before, so do confide in her and ask her advice. If she seems unwilling to help then try someone else. But don't suffer in silence. No one, man or woman, has a right to treat you like this.

VIOLENT RELATIONSHIPS

In some relationships violence becomes almost a language of love. The victim, usually the woman, dreads the next outburst but feels deep down that it's somehow her fault. She tries her utmost to keep things running happily, fearing that by saying or doing the wrong thing her partner will turn on her with an uncontrollable outburst of violence. Afterwards, he will be very sorry, saying how he can't forgive himself and how much he loves her and she will feel comforted and secure. But the idea that it was all somehow her fault will be reinforced.

These are two stories of girls who found themselves in this kind of situation.

Sheila's Story

I was 14 when I first met Jamie. He was the most gorgeous guy I had seen in my entire life. I fell for him straight away, but he was 19 and I was rather overweight so I didn't think I had any chance. But over the next few weeks we all hung around together and he eventually asked me out.

From then on we did everything together. After only one week he looked me in the eye and said one day we would be married. That first year was the happiest of my life and we grew closer and closer. I couldn't concentrate at school but kept staring out of the window counting the minutes before we would see each other. Jamie kept taking sickies off work so we could spend more time together.

We had a very strong bond that even to this day I know I will never share with anyone else.

Two years after we met, things started to go wrong. We were both good pool players (one of the many things we had in common) and were practising in the back room of my house. I had cheated as a joke and moved one of the balls and all of a sudden, without warning, he walked over to me, put his arms around my chest and picked me up with his elbows digging into my ribs. He did karate and knew how to hurt if he wanted to, though he had never before laid a finger on me. I cried with pain as I felt my ribs being crushed, then he put me down and started to cry himself, saying he was sorry and it would never happen again. I believed he was sorry and forgave him but things never went back to how they were.

The violence happened repeatedly, sometimes two or three times a week. Usually it was nothing too serious, just the odd cut or bruise, but sometimes it would be a punch. Every time he would say he was sorry and I would forgive him, hoping it would be the last time. But of course it never was. I did try to leave him at first, but he became more violent, and as I still loved him it became part of everyday life. I tried everything to make him stop, being violent back, crying, threatening to tell the police, and we separated on many occasions for the odd day, but every time he would come back saying he was sorry.

I asked him why he did it and he said he didn't know. Then he started blaming me, saying it was my fault and I guess that after a bit I started to believe it. The physical pain no longer hurt but the mental pain cut very deep. The only time I could escape was when I went to bed crying myself to sleep. But I held on to the hope that one day the man I loved would pull through and we could go back to the wonderful relationship we once had.

Still things got worse and looking back I must have been mad to stay with him as long as I did. He started getting violent with my mother and threatening her. She hated him and tried to ban him from the house but I always begged her to let him back in, saying she would ruin my life if she didn't. Then he lost his job and began borrowing money from me. He started lying to me about things, but when he began forcing me sexually it was the last resort. I told him I didn't want to see him again but he burst into tears and said he would change. I knew it was just more lies and if I didn't break free now I would never have the strength to do it.

It was very hard to adjust to life without him. I was 19 and we'd been together for five years. The worst part was he kept coming back begging me to give him another chance. It was so tempting to fall back into the trap. I started sleeping round. I hated men and it made me feel back in charge as I could decide who I wanted to sleep with, but there was absolutely no feeling in me towards them. I got myself a reputation of being a slag and because of this I started drinking heavily. I thought my problems were over when I separated from Jamie, but he affected me more than I knew.

Sheila, aged 22

Polly's Story

I never got on with my parents, so when I was raped by four lads when I was 13 I didn't tell anyone. My mum and dad thought I was just having a teenage tantrum. I withdrew into myself, hating myself. I was convinced I was fat and ugly and that everyone hated me.

When I was 15 I met Martin at school and he asked me out. I was so happy that at last there was somebody to love me. At first it was fine but then it came out that he didn't like my hair – so I shaved it all off. He didn't like my clothes or my make-up. I was fat and ugly again. Actually I was 5'6" and weighed eight stone, but when he said it I was convinced that I was fat. If Martin saw other lads looking at me it was always 'because I was so ugly'. I believed him.

When I was 16 Martin told me to go on the pill so I did. Then *he* had sex. He paid no attention to me and it did nothing for me. I decided to tell him about the time when I had been raped. He was the first person I had ever told. He took me back to the place where it had happened and did it to me again. When I cried he hit me.

From then on I had a new black eye every week. I told everyone I walked into doors and stuff. He burned my hand with a light bulb. I still have the scars there, and on my legs, arms and face, but mostly in my heart. He beat me up. He raped me, cheated on me and I loved him. Once my period was a day late and he thought I was pregnant, so he kicked me in the stomach until I blacked out. I was too scared to leave him, so I took three overdoses and slashed myself with razors. I hated myself.

It was only when I was 17 that I met my present boyfriend. I told him how Martin hit me, and he looked after me. Eventually I moved away from home and now live in a different town. I still feel sick and nervous when I go back to visit my family, but I know that Martin will never hit me again. It's taken me five years to get over this and I'm still in counselling now, but I'm getting there. I don't feel raped every time I make love and I am in control. I was in a situation I knew I had to get out of, but I had no one to turn to. I can't believe now that I tried to kill myself because of him.

Polly, aged 23

You can see from these stories how both girls were isolated from their friends and their families by their boyfriends. Martin convinced Polly that she was fat and ugly and that no one else could love her, so she turned to him more and more. He was using these lies to keep her under his control and every time she tried to break away he would punish her.

Sheila's boyfriend went through the well-known cycle of hitting her and then apologizing effusively. Sheila came to feel that it was her fault and that if he hurt her then she somehow deserved it. Both girls talk about the trap they were caught in and how difficult it was to get out. They knew they had to break free and although they were in such pain, they both believed that their boyfriend was the only person who could ever love them. Their self-images and their dignity had been destroyed. They couldn't believe they could exist on their own or would ever find relationships with anyone else.

Escape from violence

The key to escape is to tell someone else what is going on. Polly met another man who cared for her and listened, but she could equally have confided in a close friend or family member. Abused people are often reluctant to tell the truth about what is happening to them (Polly walked into 'doors' every week), but if they can bring themselves to disclose the truth to someone they trust, the shocked reaction is sometimes enough to motivate them to make a break. In other words you can persuade yourself that all manner of things are normal but when you confide in someone else you start to see things through their eyes and suddenly it doesn't seem so 'normal' any more.

SHE'S RIGHT – THIS CAN'T BE NORMAL...

Luckily there are also good, supportive services available. The Women's Aid Federation helps women, married or single, who are in abusive relationships. They give support and counselling and can also find victims a safe house away from their abuser. For more information see 'Resources'.

The most significant point from these stories is that both girls, although shocked when the violence started, agreed to continue the relationship. They kept telling themselves that things would get better. But they didn't. The fact is that once a man becomes violent he's likely to continue being violent.

Sometimes it dates back to his childhood where his parents or guardians were violent to him. He genuinely confuses violence with love and caring. But that is his problem and it won't go away until he chooses to get help for it. The moral is that if your boyfriend or husband starts being violent with you, you need to get help and, preferably you need to get out. In some cases cures are possible, but the abuser has to want to get better. Crying and promising that things will be different isn't enough. *If he's not prepared to get help, then you must get out*.

SEXUAL ABUSE

Sexual abuse is another form of abuse of power. Again it's usually someone older or more powerful who uses their position to force the victim into doing what they want. The threat of discovery is often used against the victim – because once they've had sexual contact with their abuser they feel scared and dirty and fearful that anyone might find out. The abuser uses this to draw them deeper into the secret and keep them where they can be controlled.

My friend's granddad has been 'touching' me and my friend. I suppose it's our fault because we get money for letting him do it. We have both had about £30 out of him. We regret it greatly. The first time we didn't really know what we were doing until afterwards. And we both said we'd never do it again. But the second time was more serious. We'd said we weren't going to go too far, but we went further than the first time so we

stopped seeing him. Now we're scared to tell anyone in case we get put into care.

Two worried 12-year-olds

There's this bloke who runs our local bike shop who keeps being really friendly to me. I go in most weekends and he's asked me several times to stay behind and go upstairs with him. The first time I did it he tried to touch me and I was shocked and ran home, but the next time he said there'd be something in it for me and offered to give me a really good deal on a bike. I went upstairs with him and he messed about with me a bit. It wasn't too bad at the time but I felt dirty afterwards. Now he says if I don't keep on doing it he'll tell everyone that I'm a poofter. I'm really scared.

John, aged 15

In both these cases the young people knew that what they were being asked to do wasn't quite right but they were also being offered a pretty hefty bribe. It's hard to say no to that kind of thing, particularly when it's from someone you like and trust. After all, they like you and they obviously care for you so they can't be going to do anything that would hurt you, can they? But of course, in each case the adult is only thinking of what they will get out of it themselves. They offer money, discounts or favours, so that they can get what they want. And, like John, once you've done it one time you're terrified that other people might find out. After all, you might reason, it's not as though you were raped, is it? You were offered something and you took it, and in return you let the other person touch and use your body.

But it isn't as simple as that. In each case the abuser was taking control away from the young person and forcing them by bribery to do something that was against their better judgement. *Sexual abuse depends on the victims staying silent*. It depends on the victim feeling dirty and guilty about what has taken place. It depends on the victim's fear.

The two girls were scared of being put into care and this, together with the shame of having accepted the money, meant they weren't going to tell anyone what had happened.

Luckily because we now know that sexual abuse is so common, there are people you can contact who will listen to you and will believe you. Most famous of these is **ChildLine**, who can be phoned free 24 hours a day, seven days a week. But there are other counselling services, some national and some local (see 'Resources'), all of them staffed by experienced counsellors who know just how hard it is to ask for help and admit what has been going on. No matter what favours you have been offered or might have accepted, you are not going to be blamed. Counsellors understand that the power in this situation lies with the abuser, and it is the abuser who has to take all the responsibility for what has happened.

Mixed feelings

Sexual abuse, probably more than any other form of abuse, is never straightforward. If it was simply a matter of the big, bad bogyman touching and hurting you and you telling your mum and having them taken away, then life (while not pleasant) would be relatively easy. Sexual abuse, just like a violent relationship, is a trap. One of the things that keeps you in the trap is the mixture of feelings and emotions that you experience afterwards. Some people, as in the letters above, feel guilty because they've accepted money or treats. Others just feel very, very ashamed.

Knowing the kind of things that some sex abusers do, I can understand how embarrassing it is for any young person to have to admit what has taken place, but of course unless the truth is told nothing can be done. Many victims talk about feeling dirty and soiled. They can't bring themselves to accept what has happened to them and they start to hate themselves. They're convinced that no one else could ever like or love them and often withdraw from friends and family.

My friends want to know what the matter is but I can't tell them. I'm too embarrassed and ashamed. Since it happened I haven't been eating well. Last year my weight dropped to seven stone, but it is now about ten stone. I used to starve myself but all I seem to do now is eat all day. I have put on a stone in the last two months. I've been taking laxatives to help me lose weight. I know they're bad but I can't stop. I can't talk to anyone about this because I don't want anyone to find out, especially my parents. I can't talk to them about anything as they just don't understand.

I feel so dirty and it's all my fault. Why can't I just forget about it and get on with my life?

Carrie, aged 16

Carrie was raped by a family friend but she's convinced that there's no way she can tell anyone what happened. She thinks because she 'allowed' it to happen it must have been her fault. The fact that he lied to her and eventually physically forced her doesn't make it any easier. She hates herself and assumes that anyone who knew her secret would feel the same way.

Some people are very scared of what will happen to them. The two girls who had been bribed by the grandfather were worried they would be taken into care. That's a legitimate fear because often the only way to stop sexual abuse in the family is to remove either the abuser or the victim. But the authorities are loathe to make the victim feel any worse than they already do, so more and more support and, where necessary, short-term foster schemes are being promoted. For more information about this see chapter nine, 'Rights and Wrongs'.

Other victims are very concerned about what will happen to the abuser.

My dad started coming into my bedroom and touching me when my mum was ill. At first he'd just stand and watch me while he thought I was asleep, but then he began to lie down beside me and stroke my body. Every time I protested he'd tell me it was all right and that he loved me, and that what he was doing was his way of showing his love. He said it was to be our secret as Mum would be jealous, and because I loved him, I went along with it.

Eventually he started fingering me and making me touch him. I knew it wasn't right, but he never frightened me and he always told me how much he loved me.

Now it's worse and he forces me to have sex with him, but I'm terrified to tell anyone. Apart from what they'd think if they knew I'd gone along with this for so long, I'm also very scared that they'd take my dad away. I don't like what he does to me but I do still love him and I don't want to be the cause of the family breaking up. I could never forgive myself for that.

Suki, aged 17

Suki knows her abuser very well. He's her dad and, like most girls, she loves him. How can she possibly sort out in her mind the mixed feelings that he produces in her? One moment she may hate him but the next moment she's terrified that she'll lose him and be the cause of the family breaking up. It's this fear that victims find most oppressive. If they tell anyone what is happening then their life is going to change. Their family is going to be disrupted and they're convinced it will be all their fault. I find the saddest thing with sexual abuse is the way the victim takes on the burden of guilt. It ensures they stay quiet for months, years, even for ever, but they go through their lives carrying guilt, fear and incredible pain. Yet it shouldn't be like that because there are ways they can be helped.

Why didn't anyone know?

I was abused by a friend of my parents from when I was about 8, to when I was 12 or 13. He used to come and babysit for me and would follow me into my bedroom, touch me and make me do things. I hated him, but most of all I hated my parents for not seeing what was going on. I always used to beg them not to leave me with him, and they always complained about how moody I was after he'd been to our house. But they never saw what was happening.

Looking back I can see that I should have told them, but it's so difficult when you're a child. I just wanted them to know. I felt that in some way they were allowing it to happen and even wanting it to happen. I couldn't forgive them for that.

Catrina, aged 19

My father touched me and did things to me from when I was about seven years old. He worked away from home a lot, so most of the time it was just me and my mum and that wasn't a problem, but I used to hate it when he came back. My mother always went on about how I was jealous of him, but she didn't understand. I suppose I hoped it would stop as I got older, but he was still doing it when I was 15 and I couldn't stand it any

longer. I can't believe that my mother didn't know.
Surely she must have wondered what he was doing in
my bedroom at night, but she never said anything and
she never tried to stop him. If I hadn't run away I think
I would have killed myself or tried to kill him.
   Philip, aged 17

Sexual abuse, particularly incest, is the ultimate
taboo. It is literally the unthinkable, and many people
seem amazingly able to suppress any suspicion in
their own minds because confronting the issue would
be too painful. Over and over again I've heard from
victims of abuse complaining that their families,
particularly their mothers, didn't protect them. In
some very sad cases the young people had even
gone to their mothers and told them what was
happening, but had been laughed at or told they were
making up stories. But in the majority of cases they
had just hoped that somehow their mother or parents
would understand what was going on and act to put
a stop to it. But it isn't that easy.

   One would like to think that a woman would do
anything to protect her child but, as that child, you
don't know what your mother is going through
herself. She may also be being abused, or have been
abused in the past. Perhaps she's terrified of her
partner leaving, and only too willing to accept his
assurance that he will do nothing to hurt the children.
There are all sorts of explanations and excuses, but
nothing will heal the pain of the child who feels he's
been abandoned to abuse or of the parent who

discovers that the abuse was taking place almost in front of them.

Barbara's Story

Seventeen years ago I was 26 and divorced with three daughters all under 8. Life was hard but the girls kept me going. I'd look at them tucked up in bed at nights, my three little angels. I struggled through the days but the nights were worse as I had only a TV for comfort. There were no friends dropping in, and nobody can really understand that kind of loneliness unless they've been there themselves.

One night I was at my lowest and spotted a friendship ad in the local paper. No sooner said than done, I sent my details off, not expecting any replies, particularly being a mother of three children. After all, who would take them on?

To my surprise letters started coming back. I met so many men, but none was Mr Right. They didn't really want a woman with children. I'd just about given up any hope when I opened a letter from a man who stated boldly that he loved children and if we got on all right he would be a loving father to them. I couldn't believe my luck – suddenly here was someone who appeared to want my daughters as well as me.

I wrote back explaining that I had no babysitter, but he suggested that he came to see me one evening at home. Answering the door that night I drew back in horror. He was about 50 and looked crumpled and almost like a comic book 'dirty old man'. I wondered whether I should let him in, but he'd travelled a good way by bus and seemed very quiet and polite, so I thought I'd offer him a quick drink then send him on his way. But it didn't end like that, though, by God, I wished it had.

My three girls woke up and asked to come down. Before I knew it they were in the living room. They were all over him and kept asking him if he would come again. He looked at me and said, 'That depends on your mum.' They kept asking me, please could he come back, and sure enough he came night after night. I wasn't lonely any more and my children had some sort of a father.

Three months later we were married. Unpacking the case he'd brought I discovered letters addressed to him in prison. I'll never know the truth about what he'd done but I already knew that I had done the wrong thing. I had a hell of a time with him. You name it, he did it to me. For eight years I lived with this man and suffered. And like he said before, he did love children. He and my children had their own little secret without me ever knowing. He loved them and sexually abused them one by one.

Barbara, aged 43

Barbara will never forget what happened. Nor will her children. She thought she was doing the best for them, and even when things started to go wrong it didn't occur to her that he could be hurting her daughters.

Abuse in the family is unthinkable. Because of that we tend not to think of it. That is our mistake. As a victim you cannot expect other people to be able to read your mind. They may notice you're upset, and they may hear you say that you don't want to be left alone with so and so, but that doesn't mean to say they'll understand. For that to happen you have to tell them directly what is going on, and that's the hardest thing you could be asked to do. For this reason it's often easier for victims of abuse to talk to someone outside the family first of all.

Who do you tell?

If you're being abused it's vital to tell someone. Unless you do, you have no chance of escape. It's very hard to find the courage to make that statement, but it is your only way out. Choose someone that you trust, for example a teacher, a friend's parent or another relation. Tell them you have a problem and you're very scared and you want their help. With luck they'll understand that this is something serious and sit you down and give you their full attention. But if they don't listen to you, or they try and fob you off with excuses then *You must tell someone else*.

Organizations like ChildLine and the NSPCC offer reliable help to the victims of abuse. You can ring their helplines free 24 hours a day, seven days a week, and be assured of finding someone who will listen and give you their undivided attention. Someone who will believe you. Someone who won't think you're making it up or trying to get attention for yourself. Someone who will take you seriously. Someone who will help you. When you ring one of these counsellors you don't even have to give your name if you don't want to. You are in control of the situation. You can tell them as much or as little as you feel able to. As you develop a trust with them you'll feel happier about confiding the full story; the important thing is that you make a start and speak to them as soon as possible.

Calls to ChildLine and the NSPCC HelpLine are free and they don't show up on an itemized phone bill.

You can also talk to a social worker. Your local Social Services department always has a duty social worker on call and you can either ring the office or look up the address in the phone book and call in and ask to see the duty officer.

The following stories show how talking to someone can help.

When I was 6 I was abused by my uncle and it went on for four years. I kept this inside me for another five years and then told my best friend who told her stepfather. He seemed to be very understanding at the time but little did I know that he was already raping and abusing my friend and her sister. A few weeks later he was doing it to me as well.

I stopped going round to his place, but I was terrified to tell anyone. Later he threw my friend out because she had a boyfriend and she came to live with me. Eventually she went to the police and he was arrested. There was a case in court and he got five years in prison.

We had a lot of help from the Child Protection team and you can find details of your local team either through social services or the police station. I just want other people who are worried about this sort of thing to know that with the advance of technology it is now possible to have a video link in court so you don't actually have to give evidence in public, and you don't have to sense all the 'bad feelings' like you would do in court.

Pauline

I'm 18 and for 16 years I was sexually abused by my dad and other members of the family. I always believed it was my fault, but I had no one I could tell.

Eventually in desperation I talked to my best friend's mum. At first she didn't believe me and certainly didn't know what to think, as my parents were so well respected. But she listened to me and offered to help me out. She got in touch with Social Services, who said I had to be taken into care. Luckily, I was able to be fostered by my best friend's parents so I could stay there with someone I trusted.

It really is best that anyone in this situation tells someone. You can't let abusers mess up your life and that's what happens if it carries on. I am still having problems even now. I still feel guilty and dirty and I tried to kill myself because of what they'd done. Luckily I spoke to ChildLine as well. They were great and I've had counselling with them for over three years. The important thing is not to suffer in silence.

Suzanne

SETTING THE PATTERN

How abuse leads to problems in later life

Abuse may come to an end because the abuser moves away or finds another victim, or because you yourself put an end to it. But that isn't necessarily the end of the story. Abuse doesn't just leave physical scars. Sometimes the emotional and mental ones go much deeper and last much longer. A child or young person who has their first experience of sex in this way often finds it very hard to form 'normal' relationships in later life. A girl who has been abused may long to have a boyfriend, but when she finds one she could feel sick every time he touches her. A boy who has been sexually abused by a man may start to wonder if he is homosexual himself. He may be very scared of girls, or if he is able to date them, find that kissing and touching them leads to feelings of revulsion. He may seek out gay relationships with older men in the conviction that because that's what was done to him, that's how he must be.

In my work with older women I frequently receive letters from people who suffered abuse many, many years ago. As a result they have lost their self-confidence and are convinced, even if not on a conscious level, that they don't deserve a truly loving relationship. They fall into successive abusive relationships, each one confirming to their inner self that this is all they are worth. One of the saddest things of all is that many of these people have no understanding of why they live their lives like this.

My father used to abuse me from the time I was 7 until I was 14. I got married at 17, mainly to escape him. It only lasted eleven years and since then I've gone from man to man looking for a safe and steady relationship. I was with one man for twenty years, but he abused me both physically and mentally. He died and I met another man who was all I'd hoped for, kind, gentle and sweet. But he was also jealous and demanding and used to do me in mentally. I can't seem to find the right man for me. I always seem to go for men who abuse me, but I can't think why.
Vera, aged 55

I was the only girl in our house, and at 8 my father started touching me and my mother was always cross and used to beat me. I always knew that I'd leave as soon as I was 16 and in fact by the time I was 15 I was pregnant. I married the father and quickly had two further children. My husband started hitting me when we'd been married about a year, and today, while writing this letter, I have a broken jaw. I spent a week in hospital and I've told him that I don't want him in the house, but I know that somehow he'll get back. So much has happened with him, he always seems to be right all the time. He has an excuse every time he hits me and he tells me I make him do it. Sometimes I wonder if I'm going crazy.

I know he'll be round in a couple of days to see if I will take him back, but I just need him to stay away for ever.
Polly, aged 23

These women are still suffering the effects of something that happened to them as children. But it isn't too late for them to get help. Organizations like the Women's Aid Federation (see 'Resources') give support to the victim in an abusive relationship and can also arrange safe housing for them and their children. Rape Crisis Centres give support and counselling to anyone who has been abused or raped either recently or in the past. Other organizations, some national and some local, help victims come to terms with their past and to throw off the associated negative feelings. The sooner they get help and realize that it isn't their fault, the sooner they will be able to get on with their lives.

Victims and survivors

All through this chapter I've been talking about the victims of sexual abuse. But you don't have to remain a victim. A victim stays quiet and allows something to happen. A victim feels powerless. But by blowing the whistle and finding the courage to tell someone what is going on, you take the first step on the road to being a survivor. It isn't an easy transition and it doesn't happen overnight. You may need help over a long time, possibly even years. But there are more and more happy and successful survivors of abuse and many of them are willing to give a hand to others in the same position.

Some victims decide that they can cope with the pain best by burying it deeply inside them. The idea of confronting what has happened is terrifying so they force themselves to 'forget'. I can understand that this approach is tempting but it rarely, if ever, works. The person is trying to run away from the problem but they can't – because they carry it with them. They think they are coping, but sooner or later something snaps – and they find that the past is still affecting the present. They may have problems with relationships and sex, or they might even fall into a pattern of self-harm, like cutting themselves or developing an eating disorder. In other words, they have remained a victim.

Recently I was speaking at a conference on incest and abuse when Lynne, a woman in her mid-forties, approached me. She told me how she had been abused for years as a child and because of that had always found it very difficult to make relationships. She had had boyfriends, but as soon as it came to sex she had frozen up and eventually had broken off the relationship for fear of getting too close and being hurt. She had lived an unhappy and lonely life for many many years, and then one day she'd seen a reader's letter and my answer in the agony column of *Chat* magazine. The letter was from a woman who had also been abused, and I'd talked about how hard it is to take the first step of asking for help and suggested that instead of sitting and brooding about it, she just take a deep breath, reach for the phone and dial the number of the Rape Crisis Centre.

Lynne said she'd read the letter in tears, identifying very strongly with the writer. On reading my answer she suddenly thought, 'Why not?' She knew that if she left it for more than a few minutes she would lose the courage, so she picked up the phone, dialled the number and when it was answered said, 'Please can you help me, I was abused and I don't know what to do.'

That was three years ago. Lynne has had a lot of counselling and now feels like a different person. She's in a wonderful, loving relationship and is training as a counsellor herself to help people who went through the same thing. Meeting her showed me how important it is to encourage people to get help. She showed me that it worked. Thanks, Lynne.

Chapter Eight

Say What You Mean and Get What You Want
PRACTICAL TIPS

In this book I've been trying to show you ways to cope with – or escape from – tricky situations. In each chapter I've given pointers on what to look for and how to cope, but even so I know you may still feel too shy and unsure of yourself to make that first move. This chapter is about deciding what you want for yourself and then being brave enough to take the first steps towards getting it.

WHAT DO YOU WANT?

Sometimes it's very hard to know what you do want. Talking to friends or family can help you sort out your feelings but sometimes hearing their opinions can leave you even more confused. It is very hard to do anything for yourself unless you know in which direction you wish to move. Many of the letters I receive at *Mizz* are from young people who write pages and pages about the problems in their lives, only to end up by saying that whether or not they receive a reply, they already feel much better for having put things down on paper.

In order to write about something you have to sort out your thoughts, and that process can make things miraculously clearer. I'm not suggesting that everybody has to write to an agony aunt or uncle, but if you are confused about a situation in your own life it can be very useful to try organizing your thoughts and writing them down. You can do it in the form of a letter – and you could even send it to someone you trust. Or you could keep a detailed diary – but if you don't want anyone to read it, make sure it is safely locked away. Writing down your feelings every day can help keep you sane – and looking back at previous entries may show up a pattern of how things keep going wrong. A more immediate way of sorting out your feelings is to write a list of 'fors and againsts'.

Fors and againsts

Let's imagine two different situations.

Cheryl is 15 and she regularly babysits for a family in the next village. They have two young daughters and the parents are friends of her own parents. Cheryl enjoys spending time with the girls and the money she earns is much appreciated and needed. Recently however, the husband (who always drives Cheryl home at the end of the evening) has started making suggestions to her. He began by saying how much he liked her, and then a couple of times he kissed her on the cheek as she got out of the car. Last week he took a detour on the way home and parked in a deserted lane. He put his arm around Cheryl and tried to kiss her, but when she pushed him off he told her not to be silly. She then tried to get out of the car but he said she was behaving like a baby and drove her home. Cheryl feels uncomfortable with the situation but doesn't want to lose her job. Yet she thinks if she tells her parents what is going on they'll feel angry towards her or may even assume she's making it up.

Richard is 17 and he's been going out with his girlfriend, Julia, for eighteen months. Soon he'll be taking his A levels and hopes to go on to university. Richard had never really thought about what would happen to the two of them once he went away. Now it's becoming a major problem because Julia is very scared of him leaving, and is applying a lot of pressure on him to stay at home and go to a local college. As a result their time together is usually spent in major rows, or with Julia sulking and Richard trying to make the peace. He feels torn; part of him wants to be loyal to her because they've been together for so long, but he also needs time and energy to spend on his schoolwork and his friends are complaining that he's no fun and never wants to go anywhere any more.

The first thing both Cheryl and Richard need to do is sort out the *basic question* that is worrying them.

In Cheryl's case this is probably: 'Should I continue to babysit for this family?' She writes this down and then makes two lists of points for and points against.

Cheryl's List

Question: Should I continue to babysit for this family?	
For	**Against**
I like the children. I need the money.	I don't like him touching me. I'm scared to be alone with him. I don't want his wife to see him doing this and be upset. I don't want my parents to think I've been leading him on.

In this case I think that Cheryl would see how the negatives (againsts) strongly outweigh the positives (fors). She has to do something to stop the situation getting worse. On the one side she likes the job (and the money) but on the other she's scared of what might happen and how she and other people will be hurt if this man's behaviour continues. Writing the list has helped her to identify the different parts of the problem. The next step is for her to look at what she can do to change things.

Richard is also worried about whether he is going to carry on something – but in his case it's his relationship with Julia.

Richard's List

Question: Should I continue going out with Julia?	
For	**Against**
I'm really fond of Julia.	I don't enjoy all the rows and fights.
We've been together a long time.	I want to spend more time with my friends.
We've done a lot of great things together.	I want to have time to do my work properly.
I don't want to hurt her.	I want to be able to look forward to going away to university.

Richard might realize that although Julia's behaviour is really annoying and is stopping him enjoying himself and getting on with the other parts of his life, he is still genuinely very fond of her. His goal is to find some way of changing things so that the aggro stops and he has more time for himself. His next step is also to look at different courses of action available.

What can you do about it?

Making a list helps you identify the areas which are important to you and those you wish to change. The next step is to look at the options available to you for changing your situation. In Cheryl's case she could:

1. Carry on as before.
2. Refuse to go babysitting there any more.
3. Tell her parents what is happening and ask them to help her.
4. Tell the wife what's going on.
5. Carry on babysitting but make some other arrangement to get herself home at the end of the evening.
6. Tell this man she isn't interested in him and that he mustn't try anything.

As you can see, she has a variety of options but there's no single one that's likely to solve her problem. My advice would be to stop going to the house and tell an adult, like her mum, what has happened. But suppose Cheryl wasn't prepared to do that just yet. She obviously can't carry on as before, and it may not be practical to make other arrangements for getting herself home. I'm sure she loathes the idea of telling his wife, and even if she did, she still probably wouldn't be able to continue working there. She may be unwilling to tell her parents because she's worried about what they might think, so the main options left to her are either to leave the job or to tackle the man himself.

Cheryl would have to make that decision for herself, but one course of action might be to get this man on his own and tell him simply but firmly that she doesn't like what he's been doing to her and, if he continues, she will tell her parents and stop coming to babysit. Saying something like this face to face takes a lot of guts but there's a possibility that it would solve the situation. However, if it didn't, then she really would have to get out of the situation. That means saying no to the babysitting and definitely telling someone what he's up to.

Richard's concern is whether or not he's going to continue going out with Julia. His options might go something like:

1. Continue as they are.
2. Break up now.
3. Wait until he goes away to university and see what happens.
4. Have a trial separation.
5. Continue going out, but see less of each other so he has more time for his work and friends.

Looking at this list Richard will probably realize that the last option would be the best for him, but how would Julia feel about it? At the moment she's scared of losing him and that's why she's being so possessive – yet ideally he would like to spend even less time with her.

There is an obvious solution to this but, because of all the rows, it may not have occurred to Richard. The key to the whole problem is that he has not told Julia how he really feels. What he should do is try to explain what he's been thinking and ask her to help him solve the problem. He knows that he needs and really wants more time to himself, but he also wants to carry on going out with her. If Julia was able to accept the other pressures on him, she might understand that he wasn't about to split up with her, but just wanted to change the tempo of the relationship.

Remember she's also scared of how things will be when he goes away to university, and that's something the two of them badly need to talk about. Not knowing what's going to happen is always very frightening. Acknowledging and discussing the situation will probably make Julia feel more secure. Richard still has to make his point about needing more time for himself, and it may be that she will agree to it. If she doesn't, the alternative will either be a trial separation or for them to split up altogether.

SAYING WHAT YOU WANT – CONFIDENCE TIPS

The snag is that once you've decided what you really want, you still have to get that message over to someone else. This is never easy, and throughout the book I've been talking about the importance of power in relationships. As a young person you very often feel lacking in power, but there are tricks to feeling more confident and to help you grasp some of the power and control for yourself.

Step 1: Understand that everyone feels like this.

This is a hard idea to swallow, but it happens to be true. Practically everyone feels shy, embarrassed, self-conscious or out of control at some time. The people you most admire for being self-possessed and

I AM SELF-POSSESSED AND ASSURED – I RADIATE SELF-CONFIDENCE!

assured are probably just very good actors. And acting is what confidence is all about. It's a trick, an image that people manage to put across that works so well it gives the user the confidence they crave.

You do get more self-confident as you get older, but it doesn't happen overnight. I was recently talking to a very special friend of mine who had just turned 50. She said that although she'd been dreading her birthday, she suddenly felt that she'd grown up and stopped being embarrassed for herself all the time. As a result she got a new job and has started writing a book. That's absolutely brilliant, but I sincerely hope that nobody reading this has to wait until they are 50 before they get that kind of feeling!

Step 2: Decide what it is you want to say.

Obviously when you tackle somebody about a problem in a relationship there's going to be a lot of talk and probably a lot of emotion, but you should have in your mind one simple clear phrase or idea you want to get over. In Cheryl's case this might be, *'I don't like what you're doing and I'm not prepared to put up with it.'* Richard's would be, *'I'm very fond of you but I must have more time for myself.'*

Step 3: Get your message across.

The clearest messages are the simplest ones – but you also have to make sure that they're delivered in a very direct way. You may not be feeling very good about yourself but you are sure about the idea you want to get across. Standing in a corner mumbling it at your shoes won't help anyone. Looking the other person in the face and saying it directly to them makes you look and sound self-assured and confident.

Shy people find it very hard to look people in the face when they are talking to them, and this gives the impression that they don't really mean what they are saying. So, if you can't look into the other person's eyes, then focus on a point between their eyebrows. You don't have to hold your stare for more than the seconds it takes to say your key message, but holding their gaze for those few seconds will add a tremendous amount of power to your words. Practise (subtly) beforehand on other friends – it does help!

Step 4: Keep it short, keep it simple.
It's very tempting when you're feeling unsure of yourself (or when you're very scared of hurting someone's feelings) to dress up a message in lots of

meaningless phrases like: 'Well, I was just wondering, if you really don't mind, it's just that I thought perhaps it might be a good idea, perhaps, possibly if it was all right with you . . .' These are all very nice things to say, and saying them shows that you're a very nice person, but they aren't going to help. They also prolong the agony. So look the other person in the face and say what you have to say clearly and simply.

Step 5: Acknowledge their feelings – but keep going back to your message.

What you have to say is going to have some emotional effect on the other person. They may be surprised, shocked, sad, terrified or whatever and they'll almost certainly start talking at you in an effort to get you to change your mind. Stand firm. Acknowledge their feelings, for example: 'I'm sorry that this is such a shock to you, but . . .' and then go back and repeat your message. You may sound like a regurgitating parrot, but it doesn't matter. Keep on going back to the main theme. If you don't believe me, listen to politicians. No matter how people try to divert a good public speaker or politician he will always go back to his key message and hammer it home. That's how you win arguments.

Step 6: Don't get angry.

Try to keep the emotional temperature as normal as possible. If the other person starts getting angry or extremely upset, try saying, 'Please don't be angry,

this is something we need to discuss.' Say it calmly and keep on saying it. If you really can't get anywhere, then tell them you'll just have to discuss it later when they are feeling more calm.

Step 7: Find your own magic words or music.

A trick that many people use to give them an extra push of self-confidence is to have their own secret words or song that they replay in their heads to make them feel better. You need to choose something that has a special meaning for you – and something with a bit of guts.

A couple of lines of stirring poetry or the chorus from a classic song like 'I Will Survive' can give a great boost when you're feeling quivery. Choose something that has a strong beat (not too fast) because this helps you get your breathing under control so you automatically feel calmer.

Then it's head up, eyes forward, into battle!

Saying what you want – confidence tips

NO MATTER HOW COOL SOMEONE LOOKS, THEY STILL HAVE THEIR MOMENTS OF QUIVERING SELF-DOUBT.

1.
Understand that everyone feels like this.

YOU CAN'T ACT CONFIDENT IF YOU DON'T KNOW YOUR LINES !

2.
Decide what it is you want to say.

TRY TO LOOK THEM IN THE FACE. IF EYE CONTACT TERRIFIES YOU, CONCENTRATE ON FINDING OUT WHAT COLOUR THEIR EYES ARE – THAT STOPS YOU WORRYING ABOUT THE PERSON BEHIND THE EYES.

3.
Get your message across.

YOU KNOW WHAT YOU WANT TO SAY– SO SAY IT !

4.
Keep it short, keep it simple.

SAY WHAT YOU MEAN– AND KEEP ON SAYING IT. DON'T GET DISTRACTED.

5.
Acknowledge their feelings – but keep going back to your message.

KEEP THE EMOTIONAL TEMPERATURE DOWN.

6.
Don't get angry.

THIS IS YOUR SECRET CHARM. IT WILL GIVE YOU COURAGE AND KEEP YOU CALM.

7.
Find your own magic words or music.

HAPPY ENDINGS

Unfortunately, reading this book isn't a guarantee to living happily ever after, but I do hope that seeing other people's problems and how they cope with them might help you to sort out some of your own – if not now, then later. Everyone copes in different ways but the key message is not to be a victim, but to change into a survivor. You've discovered what it is that you don't want – so all you have to do is work out what you do want and how to get it. Then grab some of the control and go for it.

In the introduction I told you about some of the people who had shared their stories with me and, through the book, you'll have discovered what happened to them – all of them, that is, except Corinne (page 9). Corinne was the girl who left her boyfriend for Steve, someone she'd just met. They became engaged on their third date but then Steve started to take over her life.

Corinne's Story – continued

Things rapidly deteriorated further once we were engaged. Steve would publicly humiliate me, and he treated me with no respect. We were constantly arguing. If I wore a skirt above my knees or make-up then I was a slag, yet the night I met him I'd had on a miniskirt and ample make-up. I tried to reason that I needed to look respectable for work, but in the end I gave in.

From then on I wore long, flared skirts and a bare face. Because of him I looked drab, but I was also tired and ill from the constant arguing and was often in tears at work. I don't know why I let myself be so dominated, or why it carried on for so long when I knew it was wrong for me. I can't even say that I was frightened of him, and occasionally I managed to be assertive with him. However the times I did not stand up for my beliefs and innermost feelings far outweighed the times that I did.

Every day I 'had to' ring him in my lunch hour, and if I was late or my lunch hour had changed then all hell broke loose. Where had I been, was I lying to him, did I fancy one of the men in my office? I spent every working day in fear of ringing him late and there being another performance. I was rapidly becoming a nervous wreck and I knew it.

I would have my tea and then have to meet him in the city centre (half an hour's bus ride from my home) just to travel back to his house with him. Then he'd have his supper and I'd end up eating with him as well because he wouldn't eat alone. Everything in my life was 'had to' and 'have to'. And I was being ruled by an insignificant wimp. I was totally numb inside and seemed to just drift day to day, being put through the same mental torture by a man who supposedly loved me.

So many people tried to make me see reason, but what they didn't know was that I already had a very long time ago. I was so numb and tired but I felt there was no turning back. I can only describe it as being brain dead – what people said to me registered in my ears but did not reach the brain properly.

All the time the wedding came closer. My parents were dead worried as they knew I was unhappy and they didn't like what he was doing to me. They asked me if everything was all right but still I said yes, I was going to go ahead with it. I battled with my conscience and I knew that I didn't love Steve and probably never had, but I was frightened of pulling out of everything.

Then one day, after fifteen months of being together, I finally decided that something had to be done. I went to my local churchyard which was deserted, and I walked through the gravestones thinking about what could be done. Eventually I called aloud to my grandmother to ask her what I should do. People would say I was definitely crazy as she had died when I was only 11. I didn't see or hear anything from her, but I did feel my thoughts becoming clearer and I suddenly realized that the only person who could get me out of this mess was *me*.

Five minutes later I left the churchyard knowing that the sham had to be ended. I felt the old me returning – in control of my life again. I went to see him straight away and told him simply and clearly what I had decided. His endless hours of tears, of pleading me to stay with him, were to no avail. I just kept telling him that it was over. For once I was in control, but in fact I was feeling numb.

He wrote letters to me for some months afterwards but I never replied. I'm a stronger person now. Two and a half years later I'm positive that no one could ever affect me so much again. I spent eleven months free of relationships after we split, but I felt so fortunate to still have my job and my friends and my family's love and respect after all I put them through. Although I don't deserve it, my first boyfriend John forgave me and we're now good friends. And I've recently met someone who I'm falling in love with.

I still can't understand how all this happened but I do know how lucky I've been. It is strange that my friends have always used me as a shoulder to cry on or an 'agony aunt'. Shame really that it took me so long to listen to my own advice.

Chapter Nine

Rights and Wrongs
KNOWING YOUR RIGHTS

Knowing your legal rights makes a lot of difference when it comes to getting your own way. No matter how convinced you are that you're in the right, people are always likely to take you more seriously if you can back up your argument with a bit of law.

This chapter is an overview of the rights you have in the different situations appearing in this book. It will give you a good idea of what you are entitled to expect but I am not a lawyer and it shouldn't be taken as professional legal advice. For up-to-date and on-the-spot information you can contact many of the organizations listed in the 'Resources' section, like the Children's Legal Centre.

LIVING AT HOME

It may be tough, but while you live at home your parents are technically in charge of you. It's their house and they can lay down the law about when you should be in, how much you should help, what sort of pocket money you can have, etc., etc. You have no legal argument against this but you can, of course, try reasoning with them in an effort to reach a compromise. See chapter two, 'But We Know Best', for tips on how to do this.

Your parents are supposed to support you until you are 18 but there's nothing laid down in law about what 'support' actually means, other than that they should provide a roof over your head, feed you and not cause you physical harm. This is the bare minimum, and a lot of parents don't even provide that. Some are so bogged down in their own problems that they have no spare energy left to nurture their teenage children. That can be pretty tough on you, so it's important to find someone else who can give you a bit of tender loving care. Often grannies and aunties are brilliant for this – at least on a temporary basis, and if things are very bad at home your mum or dad might agree that you should go and live with another relation for a bit to allow things to cool down.

Parents and punishment

At the time of writing there is no law in the UK to prevent what is known as 'reasonable' physical punishment. That means that parents are supposed to have a right to slap or hit you (generally in the heat of the moment) but not to systematically beat you, punch you or abuse you in other ways. It's obviously very hard to draw a line between what is and isn't OK, and some parents certainly do overstep the mark. If you are worried about what your parents are doing to you or what a friend is suffering, you should get advice from a teacher or social worker. Generally anything that is repeated or that leaves a mark would be regarded as excessive and a social worker would take a very dim view of it.

Your nearest Social Services department will be in the phone book (look under 'Social Services') – you can ring and ask to speak to the duty social worker or call in to the office and ask for help. You don't necessarily have to give your full name or details of where you live, as most social workers will be more concerned to comfort you and gain your confidence first. But, if any action is going to be taken, obviously they're going to ask some further questions and your parents can't help but find out.

Agencies like ChildLine and the NSPCC Helpline are there 24 hours a day for young people who feel they're being abused. They can give you immediate advice and will also answer detailed questions on your rights and what you can do about the situation. Calls are free and confidential – and they won't show up on the phone bill.

Leaving home
Technically you can't leave home without your parents' permission until you are 18, but in practice, if you left at 16 and could then prove that you were living in a safe place and able to support yourself, there's very little that your parents could do to have you brought back home. That means if you can find a friend or relation to move in with who's prepared to stand up for you and support you, then you'll

probably be all right. But not many 16-year-olds who walk out in a huff are actually able to fend for themselves on their own.

If you are desperate to leave home it's always better to do it with your parents' consent and blessing. It will probably mean swallowing your pride after some of the arguments you've had, but sooner or later you may find that it's useful to continue a good relationship with them. If you leave home before you're 16 then your parents can report you missing and the police, if they find you, will take you back. If you carry on running away you could be put into care which might mean a foster home or a children's unit (children's home).

If you can't stand it at home then do try to talk to someone before running away. ChildLine or the NSPCC can be very helpful here (and are free), and the Samaritans also offer a counselling service 24 hours a day. Their number is in 'Resources' or you can ask a telephone operator to connect you. They do accept reverse charge calls (if you are desperate). It's also very useful to look in the Yellow Pages under 'Counselling' or in the front of your phone book or Thomson Directory where there is usually a 'Useful Numbers' or 'Advice' section. This should list the nearest young people's counselling centre, where they can give you all kinds of emotional and legal advice as well as putting you in touch with other agencies who can help you. If you can't find anything in the phone book, your local library or Citizen's Advice Bureau (phone book again) should know where you can go.

School
How long do I have to stay?
You're not supposed to leave school until you are 16, although in some cases children can be educated at home if their parents can prove that it's being done in a proper manner. If your birthday is between the beginning of September and the end of January you can leave school at the end of the Easter term after you're 16 – otherwise you are required to stay on until the end of May. Conversely you have a right to stay at school until your 19th birthday if you want to. So, failing your GCSEs doesn't mean that the school can chuck you out – although breaking all their rules does! If you are asked to leave your school but you want to continue your education, your local education authority should be able to arrange for you to go to another school or a sixth form college.

Rules and uniform

You may hate the rules about uniform and behaviour that are laid down by your school and think they're silly and pernickety but, while you are at school, you are obliged to obey them. Failure to do so means you can be chucked out, which, if you're under 16, just means you'll end up at another school where things may be even worse. If you have a religious reason for not wanting to wear the uniform then the school should make allowances for you, but they don't legally have to do so.

Punishment

Corporal, i.e. physical, punishment has been illegal in state schools since 1987. Nowadays there are very few private (or public) schools who use it. This means that teachers have no right to cane you, hit you, or cause you pain in any way (not including that inflicted during PE or games practice of course), although they can grab you or push you out of the way in order to prevent you hurting someone else.

If you do consider that you have been hurt at school or abused by a teacher then you should report it straight away. Tell your parents and with them report it to the head teacher. If it's very serious or if nothing happens via the head teacher you can report it to the police or encourage your parents to get legal advice. EPOCH (see 'Resources') will be able to give you and them advice.

Other school punishments should be detailed in your school rules, of which you're supposed to have a copy. One of the most common punishments is detention, i.e. keeping you in after school. In order to do this, schools are supposed to tell parents in advance, but that often relies on you taking a note home, which, as we all know, doesn't always get delivered.

Teachers and sex
Many pupils, particularly girls, develop passionate crushes on teachers and live a vivid fantasy life where they and the teacher have a lurid and sexy affair. Some pupils try and make this come true by flirting with teachers, often quite outrageously, and generally causing them a fair amount of embarrassment. Most teachers are well able to deal with this, although it's very blush-making when you look back on it in later years.

In other cases teachers either return their pupils' attentions or set out to try and have a sexual relationship with the pupil. This is completely out of order as a teacher is acting in a parental role while you are at school and any form of sexual attention could be construed as sexual assault or abuse. For more information on this, see the section on sexual abuse (page 221). If this is happening to you, the first thing you should do is tell the teacher to stop it. If that doesn't work you must report it to someone; either another teacher, the head teacher, or your parents. If people don't believe you, then keep on telling until someone does. A teacher who tried to develop a sexual relationship with one of his/her pupils would probably be sacked.

Complaining about things at school

Everyone whinges about school from time to time, but if you genuinely feel you have a grievance then go about it properly and you can often achieve some amount of change. At one school the girls complained constantly about the state of the loos. They were dirty, smelly and never had sufficient replacements for loo paper and hand towels. Eventually a group got together and drew up a petition which was signed by almost every girl in the school. They then requested a meeting with the head teacher, presented the petition along with the request that they should be allowed to repaint the toilets themselves, and offered to mount their own on-duty system to check that people weren't messing about and throwing water all over the floor at break and lunchtimes. The head was so impressed that she started her own investigations, discovered the janitor wasn't doing his job and put the care of the school lavatory facilities out to tender. The loos were repainted, refurbished and now have adequate towels, etc. – and soft loo paper.

If you have a complaint about a particular teacher, for example that they're picking on you or setting pointless or over-difficult homework, then try to take it up with the teacher first of all. They are not mind-readers and they won't know what you're thinking unless you tell them. Equally there's not always brilliant communication in the staff room, and one teacher may not realize that two of his colleagues are already setting homework on the same night, so unless you bring it to their attention (politely if possible) you'll be set impossible amounts.

If you are going to complain it's always more effective if there's more than one of you. It's less stressful for you and looks far more impressive. Make an appointment to see the teacher or head teacher where possible and don't make demands. Offer suggestions instead. (See negotiating skills, page 45.)

If you really can't get anywhere at the school you can go to the board of governors. Your local education authority (look in Yellow Pages under 'Local Government' or at the front in the 'Council Information' section) can give you details of who to get in touch with.

WORK

For up-to-date information about general laws and local by-laws, contact the Children's Legal Centre (see 'Resources') or your local town hall or education department.

Under-16s

You can take a part-time job when you are 13, but you cannot work on a Sunday, or for more than two hours on a school day, or before 7 a.m. or after 7 p.m. on any day. You're also not allowed to do anything that involves heavy lifting or carrying. Other potentially dangerous activities are excluded – so that rules out many farm or industrial jobs.

While under 16 you shouldn't be allowed to work in

a pub or bar or anywhere else where alcohol is sold, or take part in street trading unless the local by-laws allow you to work on your parents' business or market stall.

Age 16 to 18

Once you reach school-leaving age, i.e. 16, you can take a full-time job. There are no longer any restrictions on the hours you may work. However you still can't work during opening hours at a bar or any other premises licensed to sell alcohol, nor in a betting shop.

Saturday jobs

Many teenagers have Saturday jobs. The bad news is that they have virtually no rights. The laws which protect adult workers only apply to people who work full-time – that's more than 16 hours a week – and even then you have to have been working for a firm for two years before you are entitled to many of the rights of employment. So if your employer doesn't want to give you holiday or sick pay then they don't have to. There's also no minimum wage, so although you can always try and put the price of your labour up, it's very likely that if you refuse to do the job, someone else, who's more desperate than you, will agree to do it for even less.

If you're under 15 you're only supposed to work for four hours on Saturday or four hours a day during the school holidays.

Full-time work

Anyone working full-time (that's more than 16 hours per week for the same employer) should receive within 13 weeks of starting work a written statement of the main conditions of their job. It should include things like your job title, when you started working, your rate of pay, hours of work, holidays, sick pay entitlements (if any), period of notice to be given by either side, and disciplinary and grievance procedure.

Some employers try not to produce this bit of paper and in that case you should keep asking for it. When you do receive one it's important to go through it and discuss any problems you have about it with your boss. You don't have to sign it. But if you are asked to sign and you do so, then it implies that you accept the terms and conditions.

Pay

There is no minimum wage at present, and people under the age of 18 are particularly badly paid. It's important to agree details of pay and time off *before* starting a job. I know of many teenagers who, in their desperate search for Saturday jobs, took on work before discovering that they would be paid far less than they'd ever imagined. If you are interviewed for a job and the employer does not bring up the subject of money then it's up to you to ask. If you don't then you've only yourself to blame.

Losing your job

Your employer can legally sack you but they are supposed to have a good reason for doing so. This should mean that you were repeatedly late or not doing your job properly, but very often, particularly with part-time work, it's just that they don't need you any more.

If you have been in a full-time job for more than two years and think you've been sacked unfairly then you may be able to take your employer to an industrial tribunal, but you have to apply within three months of being sacked. You can get more information on this from a Citizens Advice Bureau (see phone book) or your union if you have one.

If you are in part-time work and have been working for more than a month but less than two years, you should be entitled to one week's notice if dismissed. If it isn't offered it's always worth asking for it.

Part-time workers aren't covered by much protection against dismissal but if you are told to leave, or choose to leave because of unfair or unsafe working conditions or because your employer is sexually harassing you, then you should report them to an educational welfare officer. These are people employed by the local education authority – phone your LEA for details, or ask a teacher at school. They probably won't be able to get you your job back – even if you wanted it – but they may be able to stop it happening to other people.

SEX AND THE LAW

In England, Scotland and Wales it is an offence for any male to have sex with a girl under the age of 16. 16 is known as the 'age of consent' because the law reckons that a girl younger than that isn't able to give a fully thought-out and considered answer as to whether she is willing to have sex. The age of consent is 17 in Northern Ireland and 18 in the Republic of Ireland. It varies in other countries.

As far as England, Scotland and Wales go, if the boy is over 17 then he can be prosecuted and get up to two years in prison. If the girl he has sex with is 12 or less then his offence is considered extremely serious and he could receive life imprisonment (25 years). If he is under 17 then he isn't an adult and can't be prosecuted, but he could be placed in care. In order for a prosecution to take place someone, usually the girl's parents, has to report what's happened to the police. Often the police decide not to act but there are a significant number of cases every year brought to court and, as you can imagine, the consequences are frightening and embarrassing for everyone concerned.

The law is much less strict the other way round! In the UK women cannot be accused of 'unlawful sexual intercourse', but can be charged with indecent assault if they sleep with a boy who is under 16. It's not often taken up as a case by the police, but of course many women are attracted to younger boys and 14–15 year-olds are definitely turned on by older women.

217

Homosexuality

As with straight sex the law is different for men and women. Lesbian relationships are not illegal at any age, as the law does not recognize their existence. However, if one of the partners was under 16, the other partner could be accused of sexual abuse or indecent assault.

Homosexuals (gay men) can't legally have sexual relationships until they are 18. If a man has sex with a boy younger than 18 he could technically be in serious trouble and even face a prison sentence.

However, there is continuing pressure on Parliament to reduce the age of homosexual consent to 16, as it is for heterosexual relationships. For the current situation you can check with one of the gay organizations listed in the 'Resources' section.

Homosexuality (male and female) is no longer illegal in the armed forces, but it is banned. In other words anyone in the forces found to be homosexual will be dismissed.

Sexual abuse and rape

Sexual abuse is basically the abuse of power when an adult, i.e. someone over 16, forces a younger person, often a relative or a child in their care, to have some sort of sexual relationship with them. This can include intimate touching and fondling, forced oral sex or full intercourse. In the early stages (often the best time to make a complaint and put a stop to it), it could be limited to sexy talk or suggestion or possibly the abuser exposing their sexual parts. Whatever the degree of abuse, it is still illegal and I cannot stress too strongly how important it is to tell someone.

ChildLine and the NSPCC Helpline as well as the Samaritans are there for you 24 hours a day. You could also tell a grown-up closer to home. If the first one doesn't believe you, carry on telling people until someone does. You have a right to be taken seriously over this, and a right to protection.

If a teacher suspects that you are being sexually abused or you confide in them about abuse then they are supposed to report the situation to the head teacher and from there to the police and social services. This may seem as though they are passing on your secret, but the reasoning behind it is that they have a duty to protect you. Hopefully most teachers would discuss this with you before taking any action and be there to support you through the outcome of whatever happens.

If you are being sexually abused and it becomes known to the police and/or social services either through you telling them or through the information being passed on by someone else, then they have a duty to separate you and the abuser. If he/she is someone in your family at home, then it's likely that you will be removed to a close relation, e.g. your grandmother, or to a temporary foster home. This may seem awful and make you feel as though you are the one who is guilty, but you should be offered counselling and support and helped to get back to your family as soon as safely possible. If your father is the abuser he may be asked to leave your home and promise not to visit you until after the case comes to court. That way you can remain with the rest of your family.

Whatever happens, you will feel relieved that the abuse has stopped, but you may also feel confused and upset and it's important that you have someone to talk to about all these fears and feelings. You should be assigned a social worker with some experience in this field but you can also use ChildLine, the NSPCC Helpline etc.

Rape is when you are forced to have sexual intercourse against your will. Some sexual abuse starts gradually but develops into rape. The abuser or rapist uses their position of power to persuade you to do what they want. Other cases of rape are extremely violent and may involve threats or actual bodily harm with knives or other weapons. Some rapists know their victims and others pick on strangers.

Sadly, many rape victims do not ask for help because they feel terrified and ashamed. Yet by keeping silent they prolong their own agony (and it is agony to live in a perpetual state of fear) and leave the rapist free to strike again. If you are raped it is vital to report it as soon as possible. If you don't want to go straight to the police you can phone any of the organizations listed above or you can get in touch with your nearest Rape Crisis Centre (see 'Resources'). They will give you sympathetic and confidential advice – and will go to the police with you if that's what you want.

MEDICAL CARE
Choosing a doctor
Until you are 16 you will probably have to stick with the GP your parents have chosen. Once you are 16 you can change your doctor, either by asking to move to the list of a different doctor in the same practice, or by requesting that another doctor, somewhere else, takes you on. They don't have to do this, nor need they give a reason for refusing you. If you have trouble finding a doctor to accept you on to their list you can contact the local Family Health Services Authority or FHSA

(see phone book or ask at the library for details) and ask them to allocate you to a doctor.

Contraception

The exception to the above rule is when you register with a doctor for family planning services only. The guidelines relating to contraception and the under-16s have recently been clarified. If you are under 16 and don't want to talk to your own GP about contraception you can go to another doctor and register for 'family planning services only'. The best way of finding a sympathetic and approachable doctor is usually to ask friends for their recommendation, but you can also go to the library and ask to see a list of local general practitioners. Those with a 'C' next to their name offer family planning or contraceptive services. You then have to ring their surgery or practice and tell the receptionist that you want to register for family planning services only.

Other sources of medical help

For advice and help on sexual relationships and contraception you can also visit a young people's clinic, like a Brook Advisory Centre. For further information see the 'Resources' section.

Confidentiality

Under-16s are entitled to the same level of confidentiality or privacy as an adult. In other words if you go and ask your doctor or a clinic about a sexual or personal problem – or in fact any medical topic at all – they are not allowed to pass on anything you tell them without first asking for your permission. The only exceptions to this are likely to be if they feel that you are in grave danger yourself or likely to cause serious harm to someone else. Even then they should discuss the situation with you first. If your doctor doesn't respect your confidentiality, contact the General Medical Council (see 'Resources').

It's worth bearing in mind that a doctor doesn't have to give you contraceptive help if you are under 16. They are supposed to take into account whether or not you understand the implications of the treatment you are asking for. In other words they are making a kind of arbitrary judgement on how mature and responsible you might be. In practice, the fact that you've gone and asked for help usually shows that you are pretty sensible and you should be successful. If a doctor isn't prepared to offer contraceptive advice for some reason, they should suggest another doctor to you, or you can find one yourself (see above). Either way, they should keep everything that happens secret and confidential.

Sexually transmitted infections

Many people are very scared to ask their doctor about sexually transmitted diseases including HIV (the AIDS virus) because they fear it will go on their medical records and could cause problems in later life. The best place to get expert help is a GUM (Genito-Urinary Medicine) Clinic and you can find your local one by ringing your local hospital's switchboard and asking for details of their GUM or Special Clinic. Testing and all treatment is free. All services at these clinics are completely confidential – whatever your age – and you can ask for your GP not to be informed. GUM Clinics offer pre-test counselling and HIV testing, but you can also get confidential (you don't even have to give your name) advice on these from the National AIDS Helpline and the Terrence Higgins Trust (see 'Resources').

PREGNANCY – THE LAW AND YOUR CHOICES

If you find yourself unexpectedly pregnant, you have several choices.

1. You can have the baby and keep it.
2. You can have the baby and give it up for adoption.
3. You can have the baby and give it up for fostering in the hope that you will later be able to provide a home for it yourself.
4. You can ask for an abortion (termination).

Keeping the baby

Many girls assume there's no way they could possibly go ahead and keep their child. The shock of discovering they are pregnant and the fear of telling their families seem to wipe out the thought of themselves as potential mothers. But many teenage girls make very good mothers. Certainly it isn't easy and money is likely to be very tight. But with help, it can be done. Often families are incredibly understanding and a new baby may find itself with a mum and a grandmother living together in the same house ready to dote upon it.

Even if your family isn't supportive you can still get help and advice, including sometimes a place to stay both before and after you've had the baby, via one of the pro-life (anti-abortion) charities. (See 'Resources' section for further details.)

Housing and benefits

Your local Department of Social Security (DSS) office will give you up-to-date information on benefits available to you. Look in the phone book for their address and you will usually find a double page spread listing all their numbers and centres. At the DSS office you can ask for advice in person and also pick up some very useful leaflets. In particular look for 'Which Benefit?' (FB2), 'Guide to Maternity Benefits' (NI17a) and 'Bringing Up Children' (FB8). Sometimes these leaflets are also available in Post Offices or other advice centres. You can also obtain these leaflets by writing to the DSS Leaflet Unit (see 'Resources').

If you are under 18 then you won't be eligible for Unemployment Benefit but you may be able to claim Income Support. Ring your local DSS office and make an appointment to see the officer who deals with under-18s. They will be sympathetic and able to tell you which benefits you can claim.

Most mothers on Income Support are eligible for a one-off £100 grant from the Social Fund upon the birth of their baby. Child Support is paid irrespective of other income and can be claimed weekly or monthly. (It is assessed by the Child Support Agency, who bill the father and pay the mother.) For advice on housing you should contact your local housing department (see Yellow Pages under 'Local Government'). Remember that if you want to go on the list for council accommodation you should apply as early as possible and you'll usually be expected to have lived in the area for a certain amount of time – though this varies depending on your local authority.

Pregnant women and mothers with young children do get some priority but you won't automatically be given a house or a flat. In many parts of the country you are more likely to end up in bed and breakfast accommodation. Councils have a duty to house you if you are homeless, but this may mean proving you are actually out on the street, not just that you are about to be evicted or thrown out by your family. Again this emergency housing is likely to be very basic.

You can get more help and information on both housing and benefits from your Citizens Advice Bureau (see phone book). Either ring them or go into the office in person. They are very patient and can often help you fight your way through the maze of rules and regulations.

Giving your baby up for adoption

The pro-life charities mentioned above can help you arrange an adoption for your baby or you can contact your local social services department. Healthy babies are very much in demand for adoption and you can be sure yours will be appreciated and loved. You will probably be told a bit about the potential adoptive parents, and in some cases you may even be kept in touch with photographs, etc.

However, giving up your child is never easy. Even if you decide to do it now, you may feel quite differently after the birth. Remember you still have a right to change your mind, and the social worker assigned to you should be happy to talk to you about the situation. You can get more information from the British Agencies for Adoption and Fostering organization (BAAF). See the 'Resources' section for further details.

Having your baby fostered

Sometimes your circumstances just don't allow you to look after your own child when it is born. Perhaps you have nowhere to live or things are too difficult at home. In this case it's sometimes possible to have your baby fostered with an experienced and caring family while you get your life sorted out.

Of course you can't guarantee that your local authority will automatically return your child to you when you say you're ready. All decisions are made according to the best interests of the child so they will want to be very sure your circumstances have changed before giving back your baby. Be prepared for some pretty searching questions. However this is an acceptable and successful option for some girls who need six months or a year to finish a course or sort out their lives. For more information you can talk to a social worker or the adoption agency mentioned above.

Abortion – the law

In the UK (but not the Republic of Ireland) abortions are legal up to 24 weeks of pregnancy, but because in practice it's very difficult to determine the exact length of pregnancy, abortions are rarely carried out after 22 weeks.

Even this is the upper end of the range because such late abortions are usually only available in cases of severe handicap or danger to the mother.

Most abortions take place before 16 weeks of pregnancy. In some health districts NHS abortions aren't available after 12 or 13 weeks, which, given that there may be a two or three week waiting list, means you have to start making decisions very early on. Your GP, Family Planning Clinic or Brook Advisory

Centre should be able to give you more information on the situation in your area.

Arranging an abortion

The law states that two doctors must agree that your physical or mental state would be less damaged by a termination than by going ahead with the pregnancy. Usually that means you see one doctor who recommends you for an abortion and then a second doctor, often a gynaecologist, adds his consent to the form.

You may see your GP who could be very sympathetic and able to help. But some are opposed to abortion, and in this case they are obliged to pass you on to another doctor or clinic who will be able to help you. But remember, waiting for another appointment takes up extra valuable time.

The alternative route is to go straight to a Family Planning Clinic, Brook Advisory Service or one of the pregnancy charities like BPAS or PAS (see 'Resources'). They can offer you counselling and explain exactly what is involved. Talking to one of these organizations does not commit you to having an abortion. The ultimate decision is always yours.

Abortions – NHS or Private

Because of health cuts, fewer abortions are now available under the NHS and you may find you are too late to have one in your local area anyway. The alternative is to go to a private clinic. The charitable clinics run by BPAS and PAS operate to a high standard, and although they do charge for their services they always make allowances in cases of hardship. There are many other clinics offering abortion services, but some of them charge very high prices and, in my view, they may not always offer adequate medical and counselling back-up services. If you are in any doubt, ask the advice of your Family Planning Clinic, Brook Advisory Centre or one of the abortion charities already mentioned.

Resources

General Counselling

Libraries are brilliant sources of information on local counselling services. They often have notices on the wall or you can ask the librarian for help. It's also worth looking at the front of your phone book, Yellow Pages or Thomson Directory under 'Advice' or 'Counselling'.

Remember some counselling services run drop-in centres, but it's usually best to ring first and find out about opening times and whether you need to make an appointment. However, if it is a crisis then you should always say that you need urgent or emergency help. Most counsellors will try to fit you in where it's possible.

British Association for Counselling
1 Regent Place, Rugby, Warwickshire CV21 2PJ
Send s.a.e. for details of counselling organizations and qualified private counsellors in your area. They deal with all different types of recognized counselling including sexual problems.

Brook Advisory Centres
165 Gray's Inn Road, London WC1X 8UD
Tel: 0171 713 9000
Offers counselling to young people with relationship and sexual problems, as well as family planning advice and help with unwanted pregnancies. Branches in London, Birmingham, Bristol, Edinburgh, Liverpool, Burnley, Belfast, Cornwall and Jersey, with new centres opening each year. Telephone above number for details of your nearest centre.

ChildLine
Freephone 0800 1111
24-hour confidential advice and counselling service for young people. Calls are free and do not show up on itemized phone bills.

Children's Legal Centre
University of Essex, Wivenhoe Park, Colchester, Essex CO4 3SQ
Tel: 01206 873820 (advice line 2–5 p.m. weekdays and 10 a.m. to
12 p.m. on Wednesdays)
Advice on your rights and the law.

Citizens Advice Bureaux
Look in the phone book to find your nearest one, and ring for
opening times. They give free and confidential advice on all sorts
of subjects, including where to go for further help.

EPOCH
77 Holloway Road, London N7 8JZ
Tel: 0171 700 0627

General Medical Council
44 Hallam Street, London W1N 6AE
Tel: 0171 580 7642

Kidscape
152 Buckingham Palace Road, London SW1W 9TR
Tel: 0171 730 3300
Produces leaflets, books, parents' guides and schools
information concerning children's safety – including the problem
of bullying (counsellor available).

Local Education Authority
Look in the phone book under 'Education Authorities' or in
the Yellow Pages under 'Council Information' or 'Local
Government' for details of the office responsible for your
school/college.

**National Society for the Prevention of Cruelty to Children
(NSPCC)**
Helpline: Freephone 0800 800 500
24-hour confidential helpline for children and young people –
or anyone concerned about the safety of a child or young person.

Resources

Royal Scottish Society for the Prevention of Cruelty to Children (RSSPCC)

Melville House, 41 Polwarth Terrace, Edinburgh EH11 1NU
Helpline: Freephone 0800 800 500
24-hour confidential helpline for children and young people –
or anyone concerned about the safety of a child or young
person in Scotland.

Irish Society for the Prevention of Cruelty to Children (ISPCC)

20 Molesworth Street, Dublin 2, Ireland
Helpline: Freephone 1800 666 666 (10 a.m. to 10 p.m. 7 days per
week)
Available to residents of the Republic of Ireland and Northern
Ireland. Offers confidential help and advice to young people.

The Samaritans

National helpline: 0345 909090 (calls charged at local rates).
Branches in every town in the country. They offer a sympathetic
ear around the clock for anyone with a problem, large or small.
There's face-to-face counselling as well as help over the phone.
Everything is confidential.

Social Services Departments

Look in the phone book under 'Social Services' for nearest office.
Ring to make an appointment, or walk in and ask to see the Duty
Social Worker. Can give help on family and accommodation
problems as well as practical help and advice on pregnancy.

StepFamily

72 Willesden Lane, London NW6 7TA
HelpLine: 0171 372 0846
Advice and support to all those living in stepfamilies, whether
children, parents, grandparents, plus those wanting to help
(teachers, etc.).

Youth Access
Ashby House, 62a Ashby Road, Loughborough, Leicestershire
LE11 3AE
Tel: 01509 210420 (9–5.30 weekdays)
This central office acts as a referral agency for youth counselling
services all over the country. Send s.a.e. for details of one nearest
you or ring for immediate information.

Drugs

ADFAM
18 Hatton Place, London EC1N 8ND
Tel: 0171 405 3923 (10–5 weekdays)
ADFAM stands for 'Addicts' Families'. A national service for
families and friends of drug users, offering counselling, details of
local drug services around the UK and accurate information on
drugs.

RELEASE
388 Old Street, London EC1V 9LT
Tel: 0171 729 9904
Offers advice and referral on drug and legal problems, and
emergency help in cases of arrest.

Alcohol

DrinkLine
Tel: 0171 332 0202 (6 p.m. to 11 p.m.)
National helpline offering advice and support to anyone
experiencing problems caused by alcohol consumption.

Alateen
Al-Anon Family Groups UK and Eire, 61 Great Dover Street,
London SE1 4YF
Tel: 0171 403 0888 (open 24 hours)
For young people whose lives have been affected by someone
else's drinking. Also Al-Anon which offers support to families and
friends of alcoholics.

Turning Point
New Loom House, 101 Back Church Lane, London E1 1LU
Tel: 0171 702 2300
Deals with drug and mental health problems in addition to alcohol problems.

Relationships and Sexual Problems

Brook Advisory Centres
See entry under 'General Counselling'.

Marriage Counselling Scotland
26 Frederick Street, Edinburgh EH2 2JR
Tel: 0131 225 5006
Can refer you to local Marriage Guidance services – or look in the phone book under 'Marriage Guidance'. Offers counselling to individuals and couples, married or single, with relationship problems. Some areas offers psychosexual counselling clinics.

RELATE (National Marriage Guidance Council)
Little Church Street, Rugby CV21 3AP
Tel: 01788 573241
As above, but for England, Wales and Northern Ireland.

London Marriage Guidance Council
76a New Cavendish Street, London W1
Tel: 0171 580 1087
As above, but for the Greater London area.

Unplanned Pregnancy

Brook Advisory Centres
See entry under 'General Counselling'.

British Agencies for Adoption and Fostering (BAAF)
Skyline House, 200 Union Street, London SE1 0LY
Tel: 0171 593 2000
Offers support and advice, and produces very useful leaflets to help consider these options.

British Pregnancy Advisory Service (BPAS)
Austey Manor, Wootton Wawen, Solihull, West Midlands B95 6BX
Helpline: 0345 304030 (Weekdays 8 a.m. to 8 p.m., Saturdays 8.30 a.m. to 3.30 p.m. and Sundays 9.30 a.m. to 2 p.m. Calls charged at local rates.)
Reputable charity offering advice and counselling on pregnancy (including unwanted pregnancy and abortion), infertility, sexual problems and sterilization. Twenty-six branches nationwide and five nursing homes.

Family Planning Association
2–12 Pentonville Road, London N1 9FP
Tel: England 0171 837 8542; Scotland 0141 332 1216; Wales 01222 342766; Northern Ireland 01232 325488.
Information on all Family Planning Clinics in the UK, as well as aspects of family planning and sexual health. Write with s.a.e. for free leaflets or ring weekdays 10 a.m. to 3 p.m.

LIFE
Life House, Newbold Terrace, Leamington Spa, Warwickshire CV32 4EA
Helpline: 01926 311511 (9 a.m. to 9 p.m.)
Offers counselling and practical help to women with unplanned pregnancies. Some accommodation available for homeless pregnant women and unsupported mothers with babies. Ring head office for details or look in local phone book under 'LIFE'.

NB It should be noted that LIFE is an anti-abortion charity and therefore does not recommend abortion as an option.

Marie Stopes House

The Well Woman Centre, 108 Whitfield Street, London W1P 6BE
Tel: 0171 388 0662/2585
Offers counselling and information on women's sexual health, including contraception and pregnancy. Also has branches in Leeds and Manchester.

Maternity Alliance

15 Britannia Street, London WC1X 9JP
Tel: 0171 837 1265
Information service on maternity rights and benefits.

Post-Abortion Counselling Service

340 Westbourne Park Road, London W11 1EQ
Tel: 0171 221 9631

Post-Adoption Centre

8 Torriano Mews, Torriano Avenue, London NW5 2RZ
Tel: 0171 284 0555 (Thursday 5.30–7.30 p.m., other weekdays 10.30 a.m. to 1.30 p.m.)
Offers professional advice and counselling for people who have been adopted, adoptive parents and those who give children for adoption.

Pregnancy Advisory Service (PAS)

13 Charlotte Street, London W1P 1HD
Tel: 0171 637 8962
Counselling and help for women with unwanted pregnancies as well as regular Well Woman checks. Offers post-abortion counselling.

Society for the Protection of the Unborn Child

7 Tufton Street, London SW1P 4QN
Tel: 0171 222 5845; Scotland 0141 221 2094; Northern Ireland 01232 778018
SPUC offers free educational services and runs educational campaigns to inform people about the humanity of the unborn child and the effects of abortion on baby and mother. Also information on population growth and experimentation on human embryos.

Benefits and Housing

Benefits Agency (Department of Social Security – DSS)
DSS Leaflet Unit, BA Storage and Distribution Centre, Manchester Road, Heywood Road, Lancs OL10 2PZ
Freephone 0800 666555
Ring or write for free leaflets and general (not personal claim) advice on all benefits. See also phone book under Department of Social Security.

Child Support Agency
Advice Line: 0345 133133 (calls charged at local rates)

Citizens Advice Bureau
See entry under 'General Counselling'.

Housing
Problems should be referred to your local housing department – see phone book or Yellow Pages under 'Local Government', or ask the library for details.

SHELTER
88 Old Street, London EC1V 9HU
Tel: 0171 253 0202
Offers advice, support and housing for the homeless.

Single Parents

Gingerbread
35 Wellington Street, London WC2E 7BN
Tel: 0171 240 0953
Has over 300 self-help groups for single-parent families all over the country.

LIFE
See entry under 'Unplanned Pregnancy'. This organization offers a lot of help and support to single parents.

National Council for One-Parent Families
255 Kentish Town Road, London NW5 2LX
Tel: 0171 267 1361
Offers free advice to single-parent families and single pregnant
women about the law, housing facilities, support services, etc.

Physical and Sexual Abuse

ChildLine
Freephone 0800 1111
24-hour confidential advice service for young people.

Kate Adams Crisis Centres
443 Rainham Road South, Dagenham, Essex RM10 7XP
Tel: 0181 593 9428
Offers telephone and face-to-face counselling for adults and
children who have been sexually abused.

Lifeline
The Old Bakehouse, Main Road, Hulland Ward, Ashbourne,
Derbyshire DE6 3EA
Tel: 01335 370825
Offers telephone and face-to-face counselling/support to adults
and children who have been physically or sexually abused.

National Children's Homes
85 Highbury Park, London N5 1UD
Tel: 0171 226 2033
Operates 14 Treatment Centres for abused children and their
parents in various parts of the country.

NSPCC Helpline
Freephone 0800 800 500
24-hour helpline for children and young people – or anyone
concerned about the safety of a child or young person.

Rape Crisis Centres
PO Box 69, London WC1X 9NJ
Tel: 0171 837 1600
24-hour counselling service for people who have been raped or
sexually assaulted. Volunteers may be able to accompany you to
report the incident to the police. For local branches, look in the
phone book under 'Rape Crisis'.

Victim Support
Cranmer House, 39 Brixton Road, London SW9 6DZ
Tel: 0171 735 9166
Call Head Office number for details of specially trained volunteers
in your area.

Women's Aid Federation
PO Box 391, Bristol BS99 7WS
Tel: 01272 633542 (weekdays 10.30 a.m. to 4 p.m., and 7–10 p.m.)
Can provide safe and secret temporary refuge for women
and their children who are threatened by mental, emotional or
physical violence, harassment or sexual abuse.

Gays, lesbians and sexual identity problems

The Albany Trust
The Art of Health and Yoga Centre, 280 Balham High Road,
London SW17 7AL
Tel: 0181 767 1827
Offers counselling for all types of relationship and sexual identity
problems. Branches in London, Birmingham, Brighton, Guildford
and Hove.

Lesbian and Gay Employment Rights (LAGER)
Leroy House, Unit 1G, 436 Essex Road, London N1 3QP
Tel: 0171 704 6066 (gay and general info) and 0171 704 8066 (les-
bian info)
Open 11–5 weekdays. Helps gays in and out of work and fights
discrimination.

Lesbian and Gay Switchboard
BM Switchboard, London WC1N 3XX
Tel: 0171 837 7324
24-hour information and help for lesbians and gays. Other switchboards operate all over the country – look in local press for details or ring London switchboard and ask for your local number.

Lesbian and Gay Youth Movement
LYGB, BM/GYM, London WC1N 3XX
Tel: 0181 317 9690 (Fridays 6–9 p.m.)
Can refer you to local Gay Youth movements all over the country. Enclose s.a.e.

London Friend
86 Caledonian Road, London N1 9DN
Tel: 0171 837 3337 (7.30–10 p.m. weekdays)
Women's Helpline: 0171 837 2782 (7.30–10 p.m. Sunday to Thursday only)
Offers counselling and support for gays, lesbians or anyone who is worried about their sexual identity.

Parent's Friend
c/o VA Leeds, Stringer House, 34 Lupton Street, Hunslet, Leeds LS10 2QW
Tel: 0113 267 4627
Organization for parents of gays, lesbians and bisexuals.

Sexually Transmitted Diseases and HIV

STD Clinics
(also called GUM – Genito-Urinary Medicine – or Special Clinics in some areas)
Phone your local hospital switchboard and ask for details of the nearest Special Clinic. Most run an appointments system – you are given a number so the doctor won't call your name in the waiting room. Tests and treatment are free and all services are completely confidential, whatever your age – you can even ask for your GP not to be informed.

AIDS Helplines
National: 0800 567123 (24-hour freephone service)
Welsh AIDS Helpline: 01222 223443 (7–10 p.m. weekdays)
Northern Ireland AIDS Helpline: 0800 326117 (10 a.m. to 1 p.m.
Tues and Thurs; 2–5 p.m. Sat)

Body Positive
Tel: 0171 373 9124 (7–10 p.m. weekdays, 4–10 p.m. weekends)
Support for people with HIV and AIDS – many counsellors have
AIDS themselves.

Positively Healthy
PO Box 71, Richmond, Surrey TW9 3DJ
Tel: 0181 878 6443
Self-help group encouraging a positive approach to coping with
HIV or AIDS.

Positively Women
5 Sebastian Street, London EC1V OHE
Tel: 0171 713 0222 (10–5)
Women offering support, counselling and information to women
with HIV or AIDS.

Positive Youth
Tel: 0171 373 7547 (10–6 weekdays)
Support for young people with HIV and AIDS.

Terrence Higgins Trust
52–54 Gray's Inn Road, London WC1X 8JU
Helpline: 0171 242 1010 (3–10 p.m. daily)
Legal Line: 0171 405 2381 (7–10 p.m. Wednesdays)
Information and support for anyone with HIV or AIDS.